SOCIAL MEDIA MUSINGS

Book 4

GEORGE WAAS

authorHOUSE®

AuthorHouse™
1663 Liberty Drive
Bloomington, IN 47403
www.authorhouse.com
Phone: 833-262-8899

Published by AuthorHouse 12/06/2022

ISBN: 978-1-6655-7742-7 (sc)
ISBN: 978-1-6655-7741-0 (e)

CONTENTS

INTRODUCTION

In 2022, I wrote a book titled "Social Media Musings." In the introduction, I said I am the product of two professions driven by inquiry and skepticism, journalism, and law.

I noted that both professions are founded upon logic, rational thinking, critical analysis, and sound judgment. So, when I see something that doesn't make sense, defies logic, is irrational, or otherwise off-the-wall, I ask questions and search for answers.

I also confessed that I am a Facebook junkie, although not necessarily enamored with social media. There is certainly far too much misinformation, flat-out wrong information, etc., being spread on social media. And we know that "a lie travels around the globe while the truth is putting on its shoes."

In that book, I said that, for the most part, I kept my opinions to myself, or shared them with family and friends, until the January 6, 2021, attack on our nation's capital. Since then, taking to heart the note on the Facebook page that says, "What's on your mind," I've posted my thoughts and opinions about various situations on a variety of subjects. Many of my posts are quite lengthy, solely because of the importance I place on fact, analysis, reason, logic, critical thinking, and sound judgment.

I then included in my book, in chronological order from January 6, 2021, to February 2022, my posts on a variety of subjects, mostly—but certainly not all— on politics. Since that book was published in March 2022, I continued to post of Facebook, hoping to continue a national dialog on issues of great public importance, which resulted in Book 2, which was also published in 2022. But I didn't stop there. I also published Book 3 that same year. But I didn't stop there.

I hope that by this time, it is obvious that social commentary makes up the overarching theme of my posts. The purpose of social commentary is to provide discussion, including analysis, on social, cultural, political, or economic issues that affect all of us. A major theme of social commentary is to implement or promote change by informing the general public about a given problem and appealing to people's sense of justice.

And from what we've experienced over the past few years, we need change.

You don't have to be a famous entertainer or athlete to engage in social commentary. All too often, we equate fame and notoriety with intelligence and depth of thought. Having a social conscience doesn't depend on fame or notoriety; in fact, there are some whose opinions are influential solely because of fame or recognition; the reality is they haven't a clue what they're talking about. Further, as the 2022 election campaigns played out, there were several candidates who repeatedly demonstrated ignorance and stupidity, yet garnered millions of votes. Ignorance and stupidity must never become fashionable or acceptable. Enlightenment must always trump darkness.

What allows a person to offer meaningful social commentary is being sufficiently educated to comment rationally and reasonably on relationships among people and between people and their government.

At the heart of any social commentary lies an agreeable set of facts. Without agreement on observable, tangible facts, discourse and commentary become virtually impossible. It is toward that end that these musings are primarily directed.

Here is Book 4 of my social media musings on Facebook.

A COMMENT ON PRESIDENTIAL LEADERSHIP.

As debate rages over the conduct of recent presidents, it is appropriate to consider their performance against the generally recognized leadership qualities that inform how presidents do their job. Historians who have ranked presidents over the years have generally found several principles of performance, allowing them to rate them from great to average to mediocre.

World renown historian and author Doris Kerns Goodwin visited Florida State University last night to discuss "Presidential Leadership in Turbulent Times." This subject is also the title of her book published in 2018 that discusses the leadership styles and skills of Abraham Lincoln, Theodore Roosevelt, Franklin Roosevelt and Lyndon Johnson.

Many books have been written detailing the turbulent times each of these four president endured, and the skills they possessed to deal with them. Although certainly not without fault, these men exhibited the character and commitment necessary to accept the challenges of their time and move the nation forward.

Her address to a sold-out university audience was about the past, but it was also about our future. History talks to the present, telling us how we might avoid the pitfalls of the past so that we can prepare for a bright and prosperous future. But if we fail to heed the harsh lessons of the past, we are condemned to repeat them.

The focus of her lecture was presidential leadership. With this in mind, it's worthwhile to consider what presidential leadership is, and compare those characteristics with those who have held the highest office in the land, as well as those who aspire to someday reside temporarily in the White House.

Whether we want to be or not, we are all impacted by that elected official who is the most powerful person in the world. His policies that become law affect all of us one way or another. So, it's important that we choose for that office someone who meets the qualities listed below.

James David Barber, in his book, "The Presidential Character: Predicting Performance in the White House," echoes other noted historians in setting out some common leadership qualities that successful presidents appear to have in common.

They are:

- A strong vision for the country's future
- An ability to put their own times in the perspective of history
- Effective communication skills
- The courage to make unpopular decisions
- Crisis management skills
- Character and integrity

- Wise appointments
- An ability to work with Congress

The criteria have varied over the years, and historians hesitate to include recent presidents because they want these men to have more of a track record to go by. But those presidents who consistently rate at the top are Abraham Lincoln, George Washington, and Franklin Roosevelt. Others who consistently rank high include Thomas Jefferson, Andrew Jackson, Theodore Roosevelt, Woodrow Wilson, and Harry Truman. Match the criteria above with each president and the relationship is self-evident. The most recent ranking of presidents include each of these men among the top 12. Also on that list are Dwight Eisenhower, Ronald Reagan and Barack Obama.

Historians who last ranked the presidents in 2001 used these criteria:

Public Persuasion
Crisis Leadership
Economic Management
Moral Authority
International Relations
Administrative Skills
Relations with Congress
Vision / Setting an Agenda
Pursued Equal Justice For All
Performance Within Context of Times

Barber defines those characteristics great presidents and leaders have in common. There is an evident overlap between his list and the ones noted above. Some identify the same characteristic, but use different words. As you read this, compare those presidents over the past 30 years and ask how many match the criteria for effective leadership by our nation's chief executive, how many have strengths and weaknesses, and how many fail the leadership test:

1. They provide clarity.

Being clear about what needs to be done – and concisely expressing business visions and goals – is vital for effective leadership. Employees need to know where the organization is headed and what the expectations are for getting there, both from an individual and team perspective.

2. They listen and allow others to be heard.

Good leaders listen closely with the goals of understanding others and being understood. Effective listeners gain access to a diversity of ideas and potential solutions that otherwise would not have been generated. They also strengthen relationships, build trust, improve teamwork and show employees that they care.

3. They value conversations.

Effective communication is important, but it requires more than just a basic oral or written transaction between two people. Good leaders facilitate genuine conversations – meaningful human-to-human connections – and bring people together to work and gain agreement in order to achieve goals.

4. They model desired behaviors.

Quite simply, strong leaders walk the walk and talk the talk. In other words, they model the same behavior they expect from their teams. You can have inspirational quotes and company values framed on the wall all you want, but modeled behavior will always be more effective.

5. They encourage healthy conflict.

Healthy conflict is good for relationships and organizations because it challenges assumptions and creates great results. Powerful leaders allow different views to be presented and shared, and know that disagreements can open pathways to innovation and higher-performing teams.

6. They create an environment of emotional safety.

Successful organizations consist of employees who are invested in their work, which means there will be moments of joy, frustration, confusion, exhaustion, and a host of other feelings. Emotions, both positive and negative, are a fundamental part of who we are, and ignoring or suppressing them is harmful. Good leaders know the importance of fostering a healthy cognitive and emotional culture, in which individuals feel safe in saying how they feel and expressing their views, without stigma or shame.

7. They have high levels of self-awareness.

It's important for leaders to be aware of their own strengths, weaknesses, tendencies, preferences and other personality traits, because these characteristics have a significant impact on how they behave and interact with others. Leaders with high levels of self-awareness can consciously influence situations and positively affect their teams. Leaders that are not self-aware make decisions and behave in ways that can lead to undesirable or negative consequences.

8. They empower others.

Successful business leaders are confident in their own hiring decisions, and give employees the freedom they need to come up with innovative ideas, initiatives or processes on their own. Those who micromanage only serve to limit creativity and potential, which demoralizes employees and contributes to a frustrated and low-functioning workforce.

9. They welcome feedback.

Giving and receiving feedback can feel uncomfortable, but failing to do so could seriously hurt the company or organization. Unchecked inefficiencies and practices will hamper growth. Learning to embrace honest feedback with an open mind and the willingness to improve where necessary will make individuals, teams and the business stronger. Additionally, when leaders routinely expose themselves to candid feedback, it makes it easier for employees to do the same.

Compare these nine qualities with the following list of qualities for a great leader in any endeavor: vision, inspiration, strategic and critical thinking, interpersonal communication, authenticity and self-awareness, open-mindedness and creativity, flexibility, responsibility and dependability, patience and tenacity, and continuous improvement.

As you praise or condemn past presidents, use the criteria above to support your position.

GOV. RON DESANTIS PRIDES HIMSELF ON SENDING TWO PLANES OF MIGRANT WORKERS TO MASSACHUSETTS ON TAXPAYERS' DOLLARS, SAYING "WE'RE NOT A SANCTUARY STATE." HEARTLESS.

It wasn't too long ago that Republicans passed themselves off as "compassionate conservatives." Perhaps that was a reflection on those words etched on the Statue of Liberty:

"Give me your tired, your poor,
Your huddled masses yearning to breathe free,
The wretched refuse of your teeming shore.
Send these, the homeless, tempest-tost to me,
I lift my lamp beside the golden door!"

Sadly and tragically, those days are long gone, victim of a Republican Party that despises people who are different. These right-wingers gleefully turn them away, saying they aren't welcome here, and that some states and cities are not going to become sanctuary places. They forget, or are ignorant of, the definition of sanctuary. It is a place of refuge or safety. For those who proudly wave their bibles, a sanctuary is a holy or sacred place. Tragically, they have turned the word sanctuary into an epithet. The Bible teaches something far better than this.

Republicans are the ones in Congress who continue to block a path to citizenship, who refuse to reform our immigration laws. Perhaps they forget--or don't care--that many of their ancestors arrived on our shores seeking freedom from oppression, a chance at a better life in America as Americans. How sadly and quickly they forget. Or just don't care.

And DeSantis won't say President Joe Biden's American Rescue Plan helps Floridians, although he know it does. I suppose this is to prevent his supporters from suffering psychological distress of things that upset them...and upset his fraudulent campaign theme of how great a humanitarian he is and how he gives credit where credit is due. All the while his supporters continue to drink the Kool-Aid and buy his compost.

This is the current heartless version of the Republican Party. Aren't you proud?

TRUMP THREATENS VIOLENCE IF HE'S INDICTED FOR STEALING CLASSIFIED GOVERNMENT RECORDS. IS HE WORTH IT?

His message is clear: if he is indicted for illegally taking classified government records to his home, there will be violence perhaps unlike anything America has experienced before. I assume he's considering the foreign-initiated violence of 9/11 that killed more than 3,000 people. Or the domestic violence triggered by his speech to his rioters on January 6 of last year that took five lives on that tragic day, with more deaths thereafter.

This overt threat is designed to intimidate those who would hold him accountable for his actions. It is designed to put fear into their hearts. It may be readily presumed that his threat is aimed at the FBI investigators, the prosecutors in the Department of Justice and the United States Attorneys' Offices, whoever the presiding judge might be, the potential witnesses, and law enforcement everywhere who are oath-bound to protect those who are in turn obligated to do their jobs. He should know that fear doesn't work. Franklin Roosevelt made this plain in his 1933 inaugural address. We didn't fear the Great Depression, we got to work. And we didn't fear the attack on Pearl Harbor; we got to work.

We will overcome this fear by getting about the business of Democracy.

What is appalling is that this threat comes from a man who is a former president of the United States. Instead of calling for calm and allowing our system of justice to function properly and fairly, he is attempting a pre-emptive strike at the heart of our Democratic institutions. The Sixth Amendment to our Constitution guarantees the rights of criminal defendants, including the right to a public trial without unnecessary delay, the right to a lawyer, the right to an impartial jury, and the right to know the identity of one's accusers are and the nature of the charges and evidence supporting the charges. And that evidence must pass through a gauntlet of rules before being admissible.

These rights are central to our nation's ordered system of justice. They have served our nation well for almost 250 years. Yet, here is a man who held the highest office in the land daring anyone to hold him accountable for his actions under this sacred, tried and true system.

That he is putting himself above the law is now self-evident. That he fully expects his ardent loyalists to do the same, while breaking the law by engaging in violence in his name, is equally self-evident.

The question that must be asked is whether he is worth it. Will there by those who will heed his call and engage in violence if he is held accountable just like every other person is held accountable for his/her actions? Are there others who are eager to join those who engaged in violence last January 6 and who are now behind bars, or awaiting trial that will most likely put them behind bars? Are there others out there who want their lives in turmoil, possibly ruined. Do they want their families and jobs upended? Do they want to live the rest of their lives as a convicted felon?

He cares for himself and not for what Democracy means. Is he worth it?

ABOUT THOSE PRESIDENTIAL RECORDS.

Donald Trump's removal of presidential records, including classified documents, from the White House to his home has generated a firestorm of criticism of his actions as well some strong support from his loyalists.

Apart from the shock and anger generated by the FBI search and removal of documents from Mar-a-Lago, what seems missing from this hue and cry is an understanding of how our government got to this place of dealing with these types of records.

You may be surprised to know that up to the 1970s, departing presidents took their documents with them when they left the White House because they were considered their personal property.

Since the 1970s, however, every presidential document, from notebook markings to highly classified records, are required to go directly to the National Archives since these items are deemed the property of the American people.

Before these laws, there were no rules covering presidential records; presidents just took what they wanted as they were leaving office.

The rules changed for one reason: Watergate.

When President Richard Nixon resigned amid the 1974 scandal, he wanted to take his documents to his home in California, including his infamous tape recordings that incriminated him.

This would have meant that Congress wouldn't have access, and that records could be destroyed. Acting on this, Congress passed the Presidential Recordings and Materials Preservation Act, which made all of Nixon's material public property.

But that law only applied to Nixon, so four years later in 1978, Congress passed the more sweeping Presidential Records Act that has been the standard ever since. All records created by the president and his staff are deemed presidential records that must go to the National Archives. This includes all presidential material, whether it's routine, unclassified notes or top-secret national security documents. Those records are owned by the American people.

In Trump's case, there are actually two laws that are impacted. One is this 1978 law, the other is called the "Unauthorized removal and retention of classified documents or material."

Here is a rather ironic story about this particular law. When this law was passed, the penalty for violation was a fine or imprisonment for up to one year, or both. However, during Trump's term, the law was amended and signed by him, which increased the penalty from up to five years' imprisonment. So, it was Trump who converted a misdemeanor into a felony.

The irony that Trump now faces a significantly greater penalty for his actions—a penalty that he approved as president---should not be lost on anyone.

But this irony, however, is accompanied by the stark results of a poll concluded just the other day. According to an NPR/PBS NewsHour/Marist poll, more than six in 10 Americans believe Trump acted "illegally" or "unethically" by storing boxes of classified documents at his Mar-a-Lago resort in Florida. That is, 44% think Trump committed a criminal offense while another 17% considered his actions unethical but not illegal.

However, here's the shocker:

*A similar number of Republicans say they want him to run again in 2024 even if he is charged with a crime.

*Another 29% of Americans, including 63% of Republicans, say Trump did nothing wrong. Read that one again!

*Overwhelming majorities of Democrats (93%) and independents (65%) say the former president did something illegal or unethical, but just 5% of Republicans say the same.

The law is clear on removal and mishandling of classified records; yet millions don't believe he committed a crime, and should run for president again even if charged. Presumably, these are the same folks who believe he was twice impeached for doing nothing wrong in seeking dirt to use against Joe Biden in his failed re-election bid, or in instigating a riot at the capital to prevent the constitutionally mandated certification of the Electoral College vote in favor of Biden. I suppose the rule of law is what others have to follow; it doesn't apply to Trump and his followers. Whether this is an indicator of a failure of our education system is for another day.

Why did former presidents want to take records after leaving office? "Early on, presidents like John Adams and Thomas Jefferson were very attuned to their place in history and their legacy," said presidential historian Lindsay Chervinsky, the author of The Cabinet: George Washington and the Creation of an American Institution. "And so they were very thoughtful about maintaining their documents, cataloging their documents, and then, of course, sort of making sure that what remained was what they wanted to remain. So that also includes some erasure."

And after President Franklin Roosevelt opened his library in 1941, every president wanted to have his records for his library, or to write his memoirs.

Why was the federal government concerned about Trump's removal? Throughout his presidency, stories surfaced about Trump's handling of documents. There were comments that he didn't like to read them, and there were reports that he would sometimes rip them up or even flush them down the toilet. Further, Trump talked about, or tweeted, sensitive information that was believed to be classified. Such material was also reportedly shared with people who did not have the authorization to read it.

According to National Archives experts, before Trump, outgoing presidents were cooperative with the records retention process. There were a few minor situations where, for example, a former president might be asked to turn over a small gift he had received while in office. There have been a few cases involving former presidential aides. In one instance, Sandy Berger, who had served as the national security adviser to President Bill Clinton, was accused of smuggling classified documents out of the National Archives in his pants. He was ultimately fined $50,000.

INDICT TRUMP NOW? LET'S RETHINK THIS.

Democrats are eagerly awaiting an indictment of Donald Trump for his removal and mishandling of classified documents. The driving thought is that this would eliminate him as a presidential candidate in 2024.

Let's assume this happens. Who does the party turn to? First up is Gov. Ron DeSantis of Florida. Young, handsome, beautiful family. Spouts the same stuff as Trump, but in a better, more attractive package. He would energize to some degree the party's extreme right wing base, but he might also attract those on the margin, as well as some independents who would fall for his charm and aggressiveness without the flaming rhetoric of you-know-who.

Greg Abbott of Texas is, like DeSantis, from a large, voter rich state. He has some baggage, such as his tepid handling of a winter storm last February and flooding a few weeks ago, but he has the right—far right—credentials to make a run for the nomination.

There are others as well, notably Arizona Gov. Doug Ducey and a few senators who have visions of issuing executive orders the way kings issue proclamations.

They also have one important thing in common: they're not Donald Trump.

Trump would certainly do more to energize and excite the far right base than the others, but as 2020 proved, the base alone won't get him---or any Republican nominee for that matter—elected president.

So, being a Democrat Party advisor, and engaging in a bit of Machiavellian strategy, who would be the most vulnerable Republican nominee against Biden, or any other Democrat candidate? Surely, those well-paid party strategists have given this some thought. Perhaps lots of thought.

The outcome of the November elections will play a role in developing a party strategy going forward. Polls are tricky things to rely on weeks or months before an election because all they do is provide a snapshot of how voters' think at the moment. Events, planned and, more importantly, unplanned between now and election day could certainly influence voter movement. Right now, polls show Biden's popularity rising, along with the party's prospects in the congressional races—something unforeseen just a few weeks ago, thanks to the Dobbs abortion decision, Trump's mishandling of classified records and party leaders' tepid response.

Of course, there's no way to predict what those polls will show next year or beyond; a strategy for 2024 must begin to take shape after the November election day. One thing is certain: a strategy for the 2024 presidential election must be considered based on what we will know in just a few weeks.

Against this backdrop, and to rephrase my question, judging from what we know now, which Republican candidate would be the easiest to defeat in 2024?

Let me add another element here. There are laws called statutes of limitations. They provide that criminal charges must be brought within a certain number of years or they can't be brought at all. Generally, the federal statute of limitations for felony charges to be filed is five years. There are, of course, many other similar statutes that provide for a different timeframe, but almost all provide for at least two or three years.

So, since Trump's foray with the FBI took place this year, presumably criminal charges don't have to be filed against him until after 2024.

You see how this could play out?

Those who want Trump to be charged sooner rather than later might want to reconsider. As the statutes of limitations show, there is no rush to charge him. The federal government could simply "Let him twist slowly, twist slowly in the wind" (a quote from the Nixon Watergate era) with the prospect of criminal charges haunting him, hanging over his head, from this point through the next presidential election.

Trump's behavior would be campaign fodder if he's the nominee; if it's another, the Democrats would have to portray him as Trumplite; certainly not as strong an attack as the one that would be launched against Trump himself. Simply put, the Democrats would have a field day running against a potential convicted felon who promises to pardon those criminals convicted of attacking the capital--among other juicy issues Trump has handed the Democrats on a silver platter.

In the real world of hard politics, a political party wants to run against the other party's weakest candidate. Many believe that in 2016, it was Hillary Clinton after her email brouhaha. Add Clinton's self-inflicted wounds with the notion that Trump would bring his business acumen to government made for a compelling appeal to the voters.

That notion has now been dashed, and going forward, Trump will no doubt run a red meat campaign like he did in 2020, only with more bile, hatred and rage at his enemies—which means anyone who disagrees with him or tries to hold him accountable. He will continue his pity party against the FBI and Justice Department until there is resolution of the classified records fiasco. And perhaps even beyond that.

So why not string it out? Why not let him pout, rage, seek sympathy, etc., ad nauseam until the hurricane finally fizzles out, until all of his hot air just dissipates? After all, people can hold onto anger for just so long. Asking angry voters to keep it up for two years is asking a lot.

Assuming a rematch with Biden, does anyone believe Trump with his immense baggage would get the same 74 million votes he got in 2020? The party base is about 30-40 million, give or take. Where would the other votes come from? Knowing what we know about Trump over the past five years, does the Republican Party believe there are 35-40 million independents prepared to vote for Trump?

As battered as Biden has been, as low as his poll numbers were just a few weeks ago, does anyone believe that a man who's served 36 years in the senate and eight years as vice president doesn't have the political skills to handle fluctuating poll numbers?

To the Democratic strategists out there, who would be the Republican Party's weakest candidate in 2024?

Come on, you know the answer to that one!

REVULSION AND REALITY

I hope Ken Burns' film "The U.S. and the Holocaust" left millions of viewers horrified and disgusted at the extent of Man's inhumanity to Man. I hope they also echo the words "never again."

It was shocking to learn that Hitler patterned his treatment of the Jews from the way Blacks were brutalized by dogs and water hoses in the south during the days of Jim Crow.

I hope this series—and others like it---are repeated again and again. Some things can't be repeated enough.

Burns' message is not only about the past; it's a warning about the present as well. If we don't learn from history's most brutal lessons, then there is the great risk of repetition.

We see evidence today of rising anti-Semitism, as well as increased threats against other minorities. Migrants have always been a convenient scapegoat of fearmongers, arousing anger and revenge against them for being "different." Promises of immigration reform go nowhere because there is strong opposition by certain elements within a political party to migrants living in America under any circumstance.

Marches by white nationalists/neo-Nazis, spurred on by conspiracy theorists and those who support them, strike at the very heart of Democracy, as does vilification of migrants.

Hitler convinced the Germans to despise the Jews. He whipped his countrymen into such a frenzy against an identifiable scapegoat that they committed acts as groups that individuals left to their own devices would have found unthinkable. It is easy to arouse a group to act than it is to ask an individual to act alone. The evils of groupthink are clear in the history of the Holocaust.

The ability of demagogues to stoke fear in the masses is with us to this very day. We hear how, if left to their own devices, Democrats would turn America into a socialist country. We are told there are terrorists and drug dealers flooding our southern borders.

Here is a double reality check: first, America has never been, and will never be, a socialist country. Second, the Republican Party will not pass any legislation to reform our immigration system because they simply don't want immigrants coming here and becoming citizens. This is why they oppose a more streamlined path to citizenship; they want it to be as hard as they can possibly make it for immigrants to come here and become citizens.

It's not the actuality of socialism or criminals tearing through our borders; it's the fear of socialism and of an immigrant "invasion" that play to a certain large segment of the population, stoked by certain government officials. In short, they create the fear and then prey on the masses to buy into it.

To be sure, when necessary, our government will adopt socialist-type programs that benefit a majority of Americans. This was done following the stock market collapse in 1929 and the Great Depression of the 1930s—our nation's greatest economic crisis born of the colossal mismanagement of the economy by three Republican presidential administrations.

Even as the FDR Administration was working to lift us out of the economic firepit, isolationists like Charles Lindbergh, Father Charles Coughlin, Huey Long and the State Department's Breckinridge Long, and others, praised Hitler, sought to appease him and vigorously opposed our nation's involvement in the emerging war in Europe. This allowed Hitler to gain strength and topple one country after another. When the Japanese attacked Pearl Harbor, America wasn't ready for war, thanks to the isolationists/appeasers who kept America militarily weak.

We see this fear today. Fear of (insert the scapegoat of choice.) Fear of "them;" fear of anyone different from "us." Those who evoke fear won't provide any facts; it's enough if the words used arouse the desired anger, resentment, hatred.

So long as people buy into the fear, the fearmongers among us will continue to spread their lies.

Here is an example of the rank irony driving the fearmongers. The proof that the fear of socialism doesn't square with its reality can be found in the number of Republican governors and senators who take credit for funds coming into the states as a result of infrastructure/climate change legislation they opposed. Their brazenness in their hypocrisy and phoniness can't be overstated. They can only hope that their supporters remain ignorant or indifferent to their falseness of their self-praise.

There is a famous quote that is relevant today, although its source is in dispute: "The only thing necessary for the triumph of evil is for good men to do nothing."

When certain groups are singled out for condemnation because of their race, religion or ethnicity; when immigrants seeking asylum are used a political pawns; when these attacks are met by silence or tepid response by many who should know better; we are reminded of this quote. Of course, many are outraged by such behavior; sadly, however, there are many who look the other way.

There are signs on the highways of our nation that say God is hurt when a woman has an abortion. I wonder if those who sponsor such signs believe God is hurt when he sees images of the Holocaust, or dogs and hoses used against Blacks in the south. I wonder if God is hurt by seeing asylum seekers flown from one state to another, victims of a naked political stunt. I hope those who express moral outrage over abortion are similarly outraged over these examples of moral depravity. But I have to wonder.

Recently, Russia's Vladimir Putin has threatened use of nuclear weapons should any nation interfere with his invasion of Ukraine. This called to mind the cries of "never again" in response to the Holocaust.

There is one significant difference between then and now, however. When Israel says it won't happen again, it has somewhere between 100 and 400 nuclear weapons to back it up.

Perhaps there's a good reason why the Arab countries who vow to eliminate Israel haven't acted on their threat. Perhaps they know what will happen to their countries and their people if they launch a full attack. Whether Israel has 100 or 400 nuclear weapons is beside the point. It can be readily assumed that however many of these weapons it has, they are not all contained within that country. That means some are housed perhaps in other countries, and in international waters as well.

Israel has made it abundantly clear that it will never again rely on any nation to defend it. If Israel is driven into the sea; if Israel believes it faces extinction, it will act on its own. After all, so its leaders say, it will have nothing left to lose.

It would serve Putin and the Russian people well to take a lesson from the Arab countries. It's called mutual assured destruction. It was Albert Einstein who said he didn't know what weapons would be used to fight World War III, but World War IV would be fought with sticks and stones. I think he knew the nature of the weapons, and he was being overly optimistic in believing anyone would survive WW III.

This to me is a subtle, underlying message from Ken Burns' series.

History is replete with false prophets; self-professed messiahs who promise to lead their people to great victory over enemies of their creation.

It seems that each generation has to come to terms with its false prophets— megalomaniacs who have solutions to the world's problems they themselves have created.

We have our own mad men today. But just as past false prophets dwell in the dustbin of history, so too will today's false prophets meet a similar fate. We can only hope that history's lessons prevent a conflagration before those false prophets meet their demise.

THE REPUBLICAN PARTY'S DISINFORMATION PLAN CONTINUES

The Republican Party's Disinformation Plan is proceeding full speed ahead.

In its much-publicized "Commitment to America," the party promises, among other things, to slash drug prices. Yet, the recently enacted Inflation Reduction Act, which has as one of its purposes the reduction of drug prices, passed Congress without a single Republican vote!

Republicans also promise to "protect and strengthen Social Security and Medicare," yet the party leadership is on record as wanting to sunset all laws for five years, including Social Security and Medicare, promising to reauthorize both if deemed worthwhile. Just like they promised to repeal Obamacare and replace it with a comprehensive health plan of their own--which we are still waiting for.

Republicans also promise to protect constitutional rights. Tell that to women who no longer have the constitutional right to choose. Republican officials believe that their supporters will continue to buy whatever they sell, hoping no one will dare question them or call them on the carpet for engaging in such hypocrisy. Only the gullible and ignorant will be fooled by this latest charade.

While the Republicans bash the Biden Administration and the extreme leftists, Florida Gov. Ron DeSantis has already asked for, and received from the Biden Administration, federal aid as Hurricane Ian bears down on the Florida coast. It seems that every time a state faces a major crisis, it turns to the federal government for help. Imagine that; Republicans bashing the federal government, only to turn to it during times of great need.

DESANTIS CALLS TRUMP A "MORON."
WELCOME TO THE CLUB

We knew this was coming. After years of Donald Trump being called a moron, idiot, imbecile, among other similar things, by many of his White House inner circle, cabinet members, congressional Republicans, governors, etc., Florida's Governor and presidential hopeful Ron DeSantis has finally joined the ever-growing crowd of party faithful who've had enough of the self-proclaimed "stable genius." Not too long ago, they were buddy-buddy, but in politics ambition trumps (pun intended) friendship.

Trump's act is wearing thin, and it's only a matter of time before his erratic behavior (to say the least) and the investigations into his conduct past and present catch up with him. Other Republicans, smelling the scent of a wounded former president, are sharpening their political knives waiting for that right moment to strike. Recall Julius Caesar...and Brutus and Cassius. Except history doesn't record anyone calling Caesar a moron, dolt, idiot, nuts, etc.

Even if Trump is charged, he still has millions of MAGA lemmings ready to vote for him. Any effort to take him down could split the party. This is not what congressional leaders want after the November elections. They want a unified party going into 2024. Their problem is Trump wants to be anointed king again, and there are wannabees who have visions of the crown themselves. Ambition is a potent aphrodisiac. Expecting Trump, who believes he has a score to settle, to go quietly into the night, is expecting the impossible. Trump may well take the view that if he can't be president again, no one in the party can be. He has never been a party player; it's always been about him.

Meanwhile, as the Republicans deal with their 800-pound gorilla in a room of ambitious politicos, the Democrats are watching to see how this internal party blood-letting plays out--undoubtedly cheering on the sidelines.

THE SUPREME COURT'S "SHADOW DOCKET" FURTHER ERODES ITS LEGITIMACY

Once again, Justice Samuel Alito, the author of the opinion overruling Roe v. Wade and its 49 years of constitutional precedent, is taking issue with those who dare to question the Court's legitimacy. He says criticizing the Court is going too far. Evidently, he believes the Court's opinions should be accepted without question.

That may be par for the course in certain other countries, but that's not what Democracy is about.

If he is genuinely looking for a reason why the Court's legitimacy is sinking among the public, he and his fellow ideologues need look no further than what they see when they look in a mirror.

Here is yet another reason why the Court's integrity is being questioned--and its legitimacy shrinking--more and more with each passing year. The culprit is the Court's "shadow docket." In recent years, the justices have repeatedly relied on unsigned and unexplained orders, part of their so-called shadow docket, to grant requests for emergency relief-- whether to clear the way for executions, to block state Covid-19 restrictions or to unblock lower court injunctions of federal policies.

When the Court fails—or refuses—to explain its decisions, this arouses legitimate suspicions. Demanding the public not to criticize its actions—either overruling long-standing principles of constitutional law or by not explaining important decisions—will not work.

Therefore, the Court has no one to blame but its ideological members who are issuing decisions without explanation that affect people's lives.

GADSDEN COUNTY COMMISSIONER APPOINTED BY GOV. DESANTIS RESIGNS AFTER KKK COSTUME PHOTO EMERGES

If this were an isolated instance of a clearly unqualified person attaining public office, it could be chalked up to inadequate vetting. But considering the number of unqualified people--elected and appointed--in office today, it seems there's a pattern here.

Donald Trump nominated several for judgeships who were found unqualified by the American Bar Association.

Congress has several members who are conspiracy theorists, spouting off the wildest and most nonsensical claims that are taken as fact by their loyalists.

Republican candidates for high office repeatedly demonstrate their unfitness for the offices they seek. As an example, you need look no further than Georgia's senate race.

It seems clear that the only qualification for office in some parts of the country is ideology.

TRUMP DOESN'T HAVE TO PROVE THAT THE FBI PLANTED EVIDENCE AT HIS MAR-A-LAGO ESTATE.

In a court of law, a person who makes a claim must prove it by admissible evidence....unless it's Donald Trump before a federal judge he appointed. Trump's lawyers made the incredible claim that the FBI planted evidence during the search of his Mar-a-Lago residence that led to recovery of thousands of pages of highly classified documents. The special master who Trump wanted appointed told his lawyers to present proof backing up this claim. The judge stepped in and said Trump doesn't have to prove what he and his lawyers are claiming the FBI did.

The lawyers out there understand this; they deal with assertions requiring proof every day.

I wouldn't be surprised if the special master resigned, saying he doesn't want to be a part of a charade. That would, of course, further delay an already delayed process of managing this latest crisis brought about by a renegade former president. Delay is precisely what Trump wants.

We are taught justice is blind, and all who appear before the courts are treated equally without regard to status. What lesson does this scenario playing out in federal court do to the truth of these teachings?

AFTER VOTING AGAINST STORM AID AS A CONGRESSMEN, FLORIDA GOVERNOR RON DESANTIS IS PLEADING FOR FEDERAL MONEY FOR HURRICANE RELIEF: RANK HYPOCRISY.

Florida Gov. Ron DeSantis is asking for billions of dollars from the federal government in the aftermath of Hurricane Ian's destruction. Republicans are well known for attacking the federal government every time they need an enemy to arouse the anger of their base. They maintain the people can't trust the federal government to consider the needs of ordinary people.

It looks like there are exceptions to the party's rant against all things federal government...such as when a crisis hits state and local governments. It looks like they can't handle a major crises by themselves, without federal help that they're receiving even after some Republicans voted against authorizing federal relief for a certain northern state several years ago, as DeSantis did while in Congress.

It's good to see him hat in hand asking the Biden Administration for disaster aid. And it's good to see Biden holds no grudges like a certain former president did for a short time until more sympathetic people in the administration held away.

It's also interesting to note how a major conflagration will make Republicans act like Democrats.

Some may think this is a cheap shot, believing times were different and things change. I suppose one person's calling out rank hypocrisy is another's cheap shot. We know what will happen sooner rather than later: Republicans will go back to bashing Democrats for reckless spending and all the other red meat platitudes that arouse their base--until the next crisis which causes them to beg for federal money from the people they condemn. At least I called them out for being two-faced. If that's a cheap shot, I'll wear it proudly.

DONALD TRUMP SUES CNN FOR DAMAGING HIS REPUTATION. IS THE POSSIBLE?

The lawyers and journalists will get a kick out of this latest lawsuit filed by Donald Trump. He claims CNN defamed him and damaged his reputation by reporting as "lies" Trump's claim that the 2020 election was stolen from him, among other ludicrous claims. In short, Trump will have to prove that he has been telling the truth about the 2020 election, and CNN and the rest of the mainstream media are the ones who are lying.

It will be interesting to see how he converts statements of fact about the election results to "lies," and that CNN knew they were lies, especially after every lawsuit he filed was soundly rejected. It will be interesting to see how he deals with statements of opinions about his factual conduct directed at a public official during his term as president, and now as a public figure. Libel law requires that a public person bringing suit for defamation must prove either that the factual statements complained of were knowingly false or published with reckless disregard for the truth. Trump will have to deal with the defense of truth and fair comment and criticism.

It will be interesting to see how he can prove his reputation was any more sullied by CNN than it already is, considering Trump's conduct amply demonstrated by the public record. His supporters will believe anything and everything he says, no matter what claims are levied against him. And those who oppose him--including more and more Republicans--never supported him anyway, again no matter what CNN reported. Assuming this case gets that far--a fair assumption considering Trump's prior failed lawsuits against the media--it will be fascinating to see how he answers this question: considering his reputation, what did CNN do that independently caused further injury to it? A collateral question is whether Trump's reputation can suffer any further by what was--and is--reported in the media on a daily basis.

And, finally, it will be interesting to see how Trump avoids being deposed under oath, particularly when he's asked about his knowledge of the election results, his culpability in inciting a riot at the capital, and unlawfully secreting highly classified government records at his estate--among other points that Trump's lawsuit has now made relevant for CNN inquiry.

We all know how much Trump loves the limelight; his love of sitting for a deposition and testifying under oath is another story.

Perhaps he's hoping his case will cause the Supreme Court to change the defamation laws to make it easier for him--and other public officials and public figures--to sue for damages. Again, assuming this case even gets that far, this is not the kind of case the Court will take to make a point about defamation law. Courts like to have parties seeking relief to have "clean hands." Trump portraying himself as a victim didn't work with any of his election lawsuits; I can't imagine it would work here.

Considering the number of serious investigations under way into his public and private conduct over the years, perhaps this lawsuit is really designed to raise money from his diehard loyalists. It costs a lot to defend against the many allegations he's facing. If that's the case, he will be successful--just as he's been in the past. He plays his base very well when it comes to raising money.

I hope the lawyers who filed this lawsuit against CNN got their fees up front and took this case only after the check cleared.

"WHEN YOU'RE RICH, THEY THINK YOU REALLY KNOW."

This is a famous line from that great musical "Fiddler on the Roof." The theme is the classic tale of a Jewish family's struggle in a Russian society that is growing more and more hostile. The line is from the song "If I Were a Rich Man." Tevye, a poor dairy farmer, muses about what life would be like if he were a rich man. He sings:

The most important men in town would come to fawn on me!
They would ask me to advise them like a Solomon the Wise
"If you please, Reb Tevye..."
"Pardon me, Reb Tevye..."
Posing problems that would cross a rabbi's eyes!
And it won't make one bit of difference if I answer right or wrong
When you're rich, they think you really know!

History is replete with examples of the super-rich being presumed to possess great knowledge and wisdom simply because they're wealthy.

The latest example of a super-wealthy person who, by being rich, is somehow presumed to know how to solve the world's problem is Elon Musk. The CEO of Tesla Motors and chief engineer of SpaceX is worth over 232 billion dollars. Married and divorced three times, he recently chimed in with a "peace" plan to end the war between Russia and Ukraine.

Musk offered three proposals: first, Russia should be allowed to keep the Crimea Peninsula that it seized in 2014; second, Ukraine should adopt a neutral status, dropping a bid to join NATO; finally, the four regions Russia is moving to annex following Kremlin-orchestrated "referendums" denounced by the West as a sham should hold repeat votes organized by the United Nations.

To the Ukrainians, this isn't a peace proposal; it's capitulation to Russia. Ukraine President Volodymyr Zelensky has vowed to reclaim all of the annexed land during the war, which has stretched on for months and has led to massive casualties on both sides.

Musk evidently knows little about the history of World War II. While Hitler was flexing his military might, threatening one European Country after another, there were strident calls for appeasement. Remember it was British Prime Minister Neville Chamberlain who, upon returning to England from Germany in 1938, gleefully proclaimed "Peace for our time" concerning the Munich Agreement and the subsequent Anglo-German Declaration.

The phrase is primarily remembered for its bitter irony since less than a year after the agreement, Hitler's invasion of Poland began World War II.

But Winston Churchill saw through Hitler. He had it right when he said "You cannot reason with a tiger when your head is in its mouth." He warned Franklin Roosevelt that Hitler can't be appeased; he must be defeated in war.

Russia found out the value of a written nonaggression pact between Germany and the Soviet Union. In this 1939 Hitler-Stalin agreement, Germany and the Soviet Union promised to maintain neutrality in the event of military conflicts with a third party and to refrain from attacking each other. Two years later, Germany invaded Russia. This so-called peace treaty, like the Munich Agreement signed the year before, wasn't worth the paper it was written on.

History is quite clear that attempts to appease a despot doesn't work. A megalomaniac who sees the world through conquest and subjugation will never be appeased. For such a person, appeasement shows weakness—precisely what a dictator wants from countries and their people he seeks to control.

Accepting Musk's proposal would only embolden Putin to eventually escalate, capture more of Ukraine, and turn his eyes toward other NATO countries.

But because Musk is so wealthy, people think he really knows what he's talking about. People pay attention if you have lots of money. If he were John Doe, no one would pay any attention to his plan. But for so many, having money means having great knowledge and wisdom. The belief is if he's smart enough to accumulate great wealth, he's smart enough to understand the problems of the world, and how to deal with them.

We've had our own experiences with wealth being equated with intelligence and wisdom. Tens of millions voted for Donald Trump in 2016 because they believed that being a multi-billionaire, he would bring his great business acumen, knowledge and skills to government at the highest level. We know how that panned out, at least so far. His years of questionable business dealings and practices, along with his conduct during his one term as president, are being exposed on literally a daily basis. A leopard can't change its spots, and an authoritarian can't mask his desire for power and control.

Money and intelligence (together with wisdom and common sense) simply do not go hand in hand.

There's another song, "Where Have All the Flowers Gone," that has an appropriate line that sums up the point I make here. It tells us that we must apply the teachings of history before we mindlessly equate the two. Recall this timeless song, and its message: "When will they ever learn. When will they ever learn."

THE FBI, HUNTER BIDEN AND DONALD TRUMP: REVERSE "WHATABOUTISM"

The FBI has leaked information that federal prosecutors believe they could charge Hunter Biden with tax crimes and a false statement regarding a gun purchase, but a final decision still has not yet been made by the U.S. attorney in Delaware.

Never mind that it's against the law for the FBI to leak such information, Republicans are already sharpening their knives waiting to take over Congress so they can launch investigation after investigation into all things Biden. They've even promised to impeach President Biden, but aren't sure what the "high crimes and misdemeanors" will look like. That probably won't matter to them; they'll just attach the constitution's required standard to whatever they want, hoping to get all House Republicans to march in lockstep on an impeachment vote. It won't matter what the Senate will do; House Republicans will have their pound of revenge.

Rep. Jim Jordan of Ohio, one of Trump's most wild-eyed supporters who's slated to become chairman of the House Judiciary Committee—a frightening prospect for those who value democracy---has already promised to subpoena Hunter Biden and do his level best to embarrass, intimidate and generally make a spectacle of Biden, turning his committee hearings into a circus. Not that this would matter to the party's base.

His threats are a direct response to how he believes Trump and his allies were treated by the Democrats. The actuality of his threats promises to be an embarrassment to democratic processes, but neither Jordan nor his cohorts care about that because his plan is red meat to the party's base.

The Republican Party no longer cares about overt lies and rank hypocrisy; for its leaders and blind followers, it's all about power and control—both of which come with taking over the House and Senate in the November elections, and the White House two years later.

But first things first. Republicans have no problem with Herschel Walker's repeated lies about abortion, and his defenders have no problem with their hypocrisy over defending him for his misstatements, gaffes and just plain ignorance of the issues, while attacking his detractors in an effort to distract from Walker's failings. So much for their high road on family values.

For Republicans, deflection is the name of the game. Distract the people as much as possible by throwing things out there that will take voters' minds off their own glaring misdeeds, and worse.

So, the FBI leak is welcomed news to the right wing as they deflect as much as they can from their leader and Big Lie champion who desperately wants to return to the White House (as well as their candidates whose most important qualification for office is that they're not Democrats. They may sound like buffoons and clowns, but they're not Democrats).

Since the Republicans like to play the "whataboutism" game, here's a bit of their game in reverse. Where are the unnamed sources in the FBI when it comes to saying there is evidence sufficient to charge Donald Trump with crimes? Unlike Hunter Biden, Trump's crimes have been broadly played out on national TV.

From his speech on January 6 stoking his mob to "stop the steal" at the capital—a lie that led to an insurrection; to his calling the attackers "patriots," giving them aid and comfort; to the several televised hearings by the House committee investigating Trump's complicity in that attack amply demonstrated by riveting testimony by Republicans; to his stealing classified government records—including information about nuclear weapons—the evidence of criminal conduct is overwhelming.

Yet not a word about whether there is a belief by federal prosecutors that they could charge Trump with multiple crimes.

Perhaps that will change once the November elections have come and gone. Of course, whoever leaked this information obviously isn't bothered by how this might influence the November elections.

Still, a leak about Biden while there is silence about Trump recalls that famous line from Shakespeare's Hamlet: "Something is rotten in the state of Denmark." Putting a more modern spin on this, something's fishy here.

The other day, Joe Biden was overheard on a hot mic saying something to the effect that "you don't mess with a Biden."

That is an interesting statement, but for me one overarching fact stands out. While Jordan and his kind can turn a congressional hearing into a circus, Biden can wield a mighty pen.

If Jordan issues a subpoena to Hunter Biden and threatens to make a mockery of the hearing process, Biden does have the absolute power of the pardon. Past presidents have used it; Trump himself used it; why not Biden?

If push comes to shove, if Biden wants to stick a dagger deep into Jim Jordan's game plan—and throw a monkey wrench into the right wing's war on all things Biden--what better way to begin to fight back than by issuing a pardon to his son?

WHY I AM A DEMOCRAT, PART II

Just the other day, I was again asked by a Republican friend why I am a Democrat. I repeated a story that I mentioned in a previous post; one that I learned about from my grandfather and father in early childhood.

My grandfather, who never went beyond high school, was a jeweler in New York City. He was a very successful jeweler, making rings and pins for people of prominence. (In fact, today I proudly wear the ring he made for me when I was a teenager, and the ring he made for my dad that became mine when he passed away in 1988. These rings are one-of-kind gold and diamond initial rings. They are my treasures.)

When the Great Depression hit in 1929, my grandfather lost much of his fortune. My dad said it was about $100,000. That was a lot of money back then. Times were tough; my dad was 20 and my uncle was 16. Grandpa had to provide for his wife and two sons; it was a struggle.

Fortunately, a few of his clients were influential people, and they used their connections to have the governor of New York appoint my grandfather clerk of the Bronx County Jail. This clerkship was equivalent to a clerk of court, handling all administrative matters for this large county jail. He served in this position for a couple of years, which allowed him to get back on his feet financially and resume his career as a jeweler. (I still have his badge in its original leather case. It's over 90 years old.)

The governor who appointed my grandfather and saved him from financial ruination was Franklin Delano Roosevelt. This is why I'm a Democrat.

There are, however, three additional reasons, all related. As a senior citizen, I rely on two sources for income: a government pension and Social Security. Before the passage of the Federal Employees Retirement Act in 1920—during the administration of Woodrow Wilson--Congress granted pensions to federal employees on a case-by-case basis. The 1920 plan led to the creation of a comprehensive pension system for U.S. civil service workers. Thus began the movement toward pensions for retired government employees on a broad, nationwide scale. It is to this that I owe my own pension.

Social Security is the second prong of my income sources. This law was enacted as part of President Roosevelt's "New Deal" during the 1930s.

The third reason is healthcare. I am a Medicare beneficiary. Medicare became law in 1965, during the administration of Lyndon Johnson. In retirement, I have both Medicare and a Medicare supplement which assures excellent healthcare as I age.

What do Presidents Wilson, Roosevelt and Johnson have in common? All three were Democrats.

Sadly, government pensions, Social Security and Medicare are anathema to today's Republican Party. There is one simple reason: the Republican Party loves big business, and big business doesn't like these programs.

With increasing fervor, Republicans have worked hard to eliminate pensions not only for government workers, but across the board. They favor reliance on the stock market, pushing for 401Ks and other programs within the market system where employees pay a defined contribution into a retirement plan as a favored alternative to the government-backed defined benefit pension system which assures a retiree a guaranteed monthly income. What is important here is that a defined contribution plan doesn't promise a specific amount of benefits at retirement, and while both employer and employee contribute to a defined benefit plan, it is the employee who assumes the risk. Re-read that last sentence.

As for Social Security, Republicans want to either privatize this national safety net, or subject it to sunset and periodic congressional review to determine if this almost 100-year-old economic lifeline should continue.

Republicans have similarly frowned upon any national healthcare program; just consider their adamant opposition to Obamacare and failure to offer a plan to repeal and replace it.

Republicans oppose any social service program that they believes undermines free enterprise—the free market system. From history, I simply don't trust the Republican Party to protect pensions, Social Security or Medicare; in fact, if they get the chance, they will repeal or significantly undermine all three.

When I asked him why he is a Republican, he repeated the party mantra: the Democrats giving handouts to those who didn't work for them; the drift of the country toward Socialism; and his support for limited government, less taxes and more freedom. In other words, he uttered the same refrain I've heard time and time again whenever the question arose.

I then provided him with a bit of history about the American economy. In 1873, America faced a great economic recession called the Panic of 1873. In 1929, America was hit with the most severe economic downturn in our nation's history. You are well familiar with the Great Depression. The third great downtown occurred relatively recently, in 2008, called the Great Recession or Meltdown.

That's three great economic crises. And who was president during these events? In 1873, it was Rutherford B. Hayes. In 1929, it was Herbert Hoover. And in 2008, it was George W. Bush. What do these three have in common? All three were Republicans. While we've had numerous recessions in our nation's history, occurring during both Republican and Democratic administrations, history's worse three meltdowns all were during Republican administrations. Remember the "too big to fail" chant during the most recent grave crisis in 2008? Consider what your portfolio would have looked like if you were invested at this time.

Remember, it's the Republican Party that wants to eliminate government-backed pensions with programs offered in the market. Re-read the paragraph immediately above to see how the economy fared under these three Republican administrations.

My friend was silent for a moment, then said I was wrong and that I supported Socialism and tax and spend policies.

I told him I support social service programs that benefit the majority of Americans, like those passed during the "New

Deal," and provided him with some very recent history, the 2017 tax cuts legislation. I informed him that tax cuts for the wealthy were made permanent, whereas tax cuts for the middle class expire in 2025.

Then I told him that all government programs have to be paid for; therefore, tax and spend is a nice cliché, but it signifies nothing. Every program requires the raising of revenue so that funds can be spent to implement it. There is absolutely nothing new here; the tax and spend cliché, while full of sound and fury, signifies nothing.

Before he responded, I asked him to tell me what programs were passed by Republicans that specifically benefitted him—programs that required taxing and spending.

Silence.

Now you know why I'm a Democrat.

THE SUPREME COURT AND THE VOTING RIGHTS ACT: HOW WE GOT TO WHERE WE ARE.

As the United States Supreme Court considers whether the last remaining vestige of the Voting Right Act of 1965 has any viability in allowing injured parties to sue, it's important to consider how we got to where we are now in terms of voting and representative government.

In 1986, the Supreme Court decided a case called Thornburg v. Gingles, in which a unanimous Court found that "the legacy of official discrimination ... acted in concert with the multimember districting scheme to impair the ability of 'cohesive groups of black voters to participate equally in the political process and to elect candidates of their choice.'" The ruling resulted in the invalidation of districts in the North Carolina General Assembly and led to more single-member districts in state legislatures.

This type of legal analysis was called a vote dilution inquiry. The Court said the existence of vote dilution caused by submergence in a multimember district is district specific. A successful claim under Section 2 of the Voting Rights Act of 1965 requires evidence that an affected minority group is sufficiently large to elect a representative of its choice, that the minority group is politically cohesive, and white majority voters cast their ballots sufficiently as a bloc to usually defeat the preferred candidates of the minority group.

This technical vote dilution standard was seized upon by various racial and ethnic minority groups during the redistricting process following the decennial census of 1990. In 1992, lawsuits following the redistricting of Congress and state legislatures abounded nationwide. In Florida, I was one of the lawyers who defended the plans passed by the legislature for both Congress and the state legislature. Those groups challenging the adopted plans argued that if a majority-minority district could be created, it was obligatory for the government to create it. In other words, if it could be shown that a district could be created in which a minority group was a majority, the government would have to create it. It is important to note here that not a single court has ever endorsed this majority-minority argument. Nevertheless, it carried sway in 1992.

The Florida legislature passed both congressional and state legislative districts plans—which were immediately challenged in both federal and state courts as not being wholly faithful to this notion. Ultimately, after much litigation, the courts adopted plans for both along the lines of creating minority districts where possible.

Now here is where the rubber meets the road. In order to create these minority-majority districts, minorities in surrounding districts had to be packed into these single districts. This meant taking surrounding districts that were party competitive and bleaching them from Democrat influence, resulting in the surrounding districts becoming safe Republican districts.

Thus, minorities got what they wanted—safe, secure districts. But the Republicans got what they wanted—more majority Republican districts than Democrat districts.

It's not as if the Democrats weren't aware of this 30 years ago. Republicans well knew the voting patterns of Democrats, including their penchant for voting in blocs. And they also knew how Democrats rely on "groupthink"

to appeal to their voters— "Latinos for _____,"
"African -Americans for _____."

Republicans also knew the Democrats wouldn't oppose their group supporters in seeking majority single member districts (and thereby bleaching surrounding districts of Democrat votes) because they didn't want to lose a substantial part of their base. For Republicans, this was a perfect situation; they knew they were in the catbird's seat.

During a brief respite from the litigation, I met with the lead attorney for the plaintiffs challenging the state plan, who was also a leading member of the state Republican Party. I told him the plan proposed to the court, if adopted, would guarantee the Republican Party majority control of both the congressional delegation and the state legislature. He smiled and said "that's the plan."

After the two redistricting plans became law, the Republicans further realized they didn't need a majority of the votes to attain control of the federal or state governments. All they needed was enough districts to gain control of the legislative branches of government. For example, today, while the Florida population is a bit over 50-50 in favor of Republicans, they control a supermajority of the seats in the congressional delegation and the state legislature. And even before, when Florida had a Democrat voter registration majority, the Republicans still enjoyed supermajority representation in both.

Republicans also realized something else: they don't need a majority of the popular vote to elect a president. All they need is enough states with electoral votes adding up to 270 to gain the White House. The last two Republican presidents, George Bush and Donald Trump, both were elected without the popular vote. (In 2004, Bush won with a popular vote of less than 51%, but he was an incumbent at that time.)

Recall that although Joe Biden won the popular vote by more than seven million votes, a few thousand vote differential in a few states would have given Trump enough electoral college votes to be re-elected.

To put it directly, in 2024, the Republicans will not need a majority of the popular vote to elect a president.

Now, 30 years later and after much revamping of state election laws to deal with non-existent voter fraud, and a conservative-dominated Supreme Court that threatens to take a pickax to what's left of the Voting Rights Act, it's proper to consider who's to blame for this. Is it the Republicans who saw an advantage based on their knowledge of Democrat voting patterns coupled with the party's mania for minority districts to appease their group supporters? Or is it the Democrats who saw what was happening, but remained silent so as to not anger their support groups? Or is it the Democrat support groups who knew what was happening, but wanted guaranteed representation rather than having to run candidates in competitive districts?

I will leave the answer for you.

THE EVIL OF TWO LESSERS?

Former congresswoman and 2020 presidential candidate Tulsi Gabbard is leaving the Democratic Party.

"I can no longer remain in today's Democratic Party. It's now under the complete control of an elitist cabal of warmongers driven by cowardly wokeness, who divide us by racializing every issue & stoking anti-white racism, who actively work to undermine our God-given freedoms enshrined in our Constitution," she said.

Sounds as if she's ready to join the Republican Party, where she'll be right at home with the election deniers, wacky conspiracy theorists, Sen. Tommy Tuberville-like racism, Herschel Walker-like family values, Kanye West-like anti-Semitism, white nationalists, law and order advocates avoiding subpoenas and seeking pardons to avoid punishment for their crimes while advocating violence if they don't get their way, and endorsers of Putin's war against Ukraine.

Yep, she'll be right at home.

IS BIGOTRY BECOMING MAINSTREAM?

In the past few days, a United States senator and a famous entertainer spewed bigotry against African-Americans and Jews. They are certainly not the first; tragically, they won't be the last.

Senator Tommy Tuberville of Alabama claimed Democrats are "pro-crime" and favor reparations for the descendants of people who were enslaved in America because they believe "the people that do the crime are owed that."

"They're not soft on crime. They're pro-crime. They want crime," Tuberville said of Democrats. "They want crime because they want to take over what you got. They want to control what you have. They want reparations because they think the people that do the crime are owed that. Bulls**t. They are not owed that."

Tuberville said this not during a private conversation, or caught on a hot mic; he made these racist remarks during a rally held by former President Donald Trump in Nevada in support of the state's Republican candidates on the ballot in November. A crowd of loyal supporters loudly cheered his comments. That what he said isn't true is of no matter; he believes it appeals to the party's base

Hip hop star Kanye West made antisemitic comments in portions of a Fox News interview that were edited out of the program before it was broadcast. His latest statements espousing antisemitic conspiracy theories and stereotypes came amid an uproar over a series of other anti-Jewish comments from West in recent days, as well as in the past.

In defense of West, a few Republicans mentioned his mental health issues. From this, are we to assume that those who harbor such bigotry are mentally unbalanced? If so—if he is unable to distinguish between right and wrong in what he believes and says--he doesn't belong on a stage making millions; he belongs in a mental institution where he can get the care he needs.

And what about Tommy Tuberville? Since no one seems to be questioning his mental fitness, are we to assume his comments reflect a sound mind? Or are we to assume that no one of sound mind would make such comments at a public gathering and therefore his bigoted comments are driven by mental issues? What about his cheering supporters? Is their cheering support for such comments reflective of a sound mind, or are they, too, driven by mental issues?

Discrimination has been with us since the dawn of civilization. One anthropologist notes that people have always been dividing the world into 'us' and 'them.' "Typically, though, it's been on the basis of language, religion, place of origin, and so on. Historically, appearance wasn't a major factor in how people were divided up. People would, of course, notice different skin and eye colors and the like, but they were treated more like differences like height and weight, which is to say part of normal human variation, than fundamental differences between groups of people. The exception here is that there are a few ancient writers (and it was by no means all of them) who tended to regard Black Africans as in some way fundamentally different from other people. This thread was later continued by a variety of authors writing in Arabic though, again, not all.

But racism as we know it is an invention of the early modern period, a result of forces including Enlightenment-era eagerness to categorize everything, increasing western political and economic leverage over the rest of the world, and European exploratory and colonial efforts pushing natural philosophers to come to terms with the range of human diversity they were discovering."

Until relatively recently, vile comments such as those from Tuberville and West were largely relegated to private conversations, usually among small groups, and usually faced condemnation when leaked to the media.

But lately, driven in significant part by actions of some politicians over the past few years, these types of comments have gone mainstream, uttered at rallies for political candidates and cheered wildly by those who support them; or offered on national news media, for the viewing audience's information and entertainment.

Where there should be universal condemnation and outrage, there is tepid response and feckless efforts to justify such vile language.

We can only hope that cooler, rational thinking heads and our better angels take control of the national conversation.

The kind of rhetoric spewing from the mouths, minds and hearts of the Tubervilles and Wests must never gain the upper hand in America.

Tuberville took an oath to defend the Constitution and the laws of the nation. He and his party leaders wax on the rule of law and law and order. Racially bigoted statements are anathema to our Constitution and laws, and are the antithesis of law and order and the rule of law.

West can be dismissed as being mentally ill, but he is followed by millions and commands a nationwide audience. If he is unable to act responsibly, that should be pointed out by those who provide him with an audience through the media, or follow his every word and deed. Mental illness must not become a convenient excuse for spewing hatred.

For a political party that espouses personal accountability, it's time for reasonable, caring Republicans to join others in categorically rejecting such hatred, declaring without reservation that such bigotry has no place at the American table.

To be sure, others have called out these statements for what they are. We await the Republican Party leadership to join them.

THIS IS THE LATEST EXAMPLE OF WHAT THE RULE OF LAW MEANS TO THE REPUBLICAN PARTY.

In her latest column, author and historian Heather Cox Richardson provides an apt description of how the radical right wing views accountability and personal responsibility. These apply to those who disagree with them; they don't apply to their words or deeds.

Richardson discusses the nearly one billion dollar verdict against Alex Jones who, rather than show some sense of compassion for his lies and mockery, continues snubbing his nose at our judicial system by telling his supporters that he won't pay a dime to those he defamed, causing emotional distress, and whose privacy he violated.

Adding insult to injury, he also asks his supporters to send him money--undoubtedly something he picked up from Donald Trump. When you're held accountable for your lies, just ask your lemmings for money. After all, they know that P. T. Barnum, was right--there's a sucker born every minute.

Not to be outdone, the right wing's darling Marjorie Taylor Greene wonders what all of the fuss is about. She says it's only words, and besides Jones has a First Amendment right to say what he pleases. Someone who has some modicum of intelligence must inform this ignorant, spaced out dingbat that the First Amendment applies to government action, not words spoken by private individuals about other private individuals. But her latest example of ignorance and stupidity won't stop her or her kind.

So, we can add Jones' actions to the growing list of examples of what the Republican Party really means when their leaders talk about the rule of law. The Republican Party is about mocking the judicial system that seeks to hold them accountable, defying subpoenas, seeking pardons, election lies, stoking violence if denied their way, stealing government records, the list goes on and on, and it's a tragedy that a once-proud major political party has sunk to such a disgraceful low.

But our judicial system has been tried and tested before. The wheels of justice grind exceedingly slow and exceedingly fine. Over time, those who believe they're above the law will face their day of reckoning. That jury verdict will follow Jones for the rest of his life. There are procedures in place for those who defy a judgment and refuse to pay. Ultimately, he will pay--just like others who believe they can do as they please regardless of what the law allows.

HOUSE COMMITTEE SUBPOENAS TRUMP TO TESTIFY UNDER OATH

The committee members investigating the January 6 attack on the capital know full well Trump won't testify.

First, he's never testified under oath about anything related to his conduct in office.

Second, he would either commit perjury or look weak taking the Fifth Amendment again and again.

Third, the prospect of having those committee members questioning him should send chills up and down his spine. Can you imagine him saying, "Who are you going to believe, me or all those Republican witnesses who testified uniformly and publicly under oath through 10 hearings?" Trump is known for many things; veracity and credibility are not among them.

Fourth, by not testifying, his minions can be fed whatever tripe Trump wants to give them, and they'll blindly accept it as gospel.

I believe the committee did this so the members can say they gave him one final chance to set the record straight as he sees it. Considering his demeanor and frequent incoherence, an appearance by him will only make the final report that much more riveting and damning.

Trump simply is not going to sit before the committee in full view of a television audience and answer truthfully and clearly under oath. We know how he fumbled his TV appearances during the COVID pandemic; how he complained about how the media dealt with him. Magnify that exponentially should he choose to testify under oath and you can readily see the great risk he would be taking.

He may try for a Hail Mary and pull what would be a shocker, but he needs to control the dynamics of any situation. And he won't be able to do that in front of this committee.

TRUMP RESPONDS: "LOVES THE IDEA OF TESTIFYING."

FOX News is reporting that Trump "loves the idea of testifying" before the House select committee investigating January 6th, adding that if Trump complied with the subpoena and testified, he would "talk about how corrupt the election was, how corrupt the committee was, and how Nancy Pelosi did not call up the National Guard that Trump strongly recommended for her to do three days earlier on January 3, 2021."

Trump also again slammed the committee and its investigation as a "witch hunt."

"The committee is a hoax, a sham, a partisan witch hunt which is a continuation of the witch hunt that has gone on since the great day for our country that I came down the golden escalator with our future first lady," Trump said. "They have no case, they have no ratings, so they have to try to do this to get publicity."

It will be interesting to see if he can get away with his present intentions to make statements like those quoted above. As this moves forward, let's see what conditions, restrictions, qualifications, limitations, etc., he'll impose, forcing the committee's hand and allowing Trump, in his mind, to control the narrative. If the questioning gets too hot, he might well storm off the stage, blasting the committee as he has in the past. He won't lose his base no matter what he does. He may figure he has nothing to lose, and he would draw a large TV audience, which he loves.

PEOPLE ARE KIND....UNTIL YOU DISAGREE WITH THEM.

This lies at the heart of our disconnect. Too many people believe that if you disagree with their opinions, you are the one who's wrong. It's an attitude of "who are you to disagree with me?"

There are generally two types of opinions: those based on fact and those based on belief. We are very familiar with the first type. Judges use this method of supporting their opinions with facts. Journalists are trained to get the facts and let the reader reach his/her own opinions from those facts.

I think the problem of disconnect arises when belief is the basis of opinions; that is, when belief becomes fact. The problem here is that beliefs are personal, whereas facts provide a common ground for discussion. Nowhere is this more evident than on the subject of religion. Religion is based wholly on faith and belief. It is also intensely personal. It is perfectly proper for a person to express one's religious beliefs. The problem arises from two fronts here: first, when that person condemns those who don't share the same beliefs and further believes his views are superior to yours; and two, when those who share the same religious views force their beliefs on others, usually through government action. The consequences of a government deciding which religion will be given priority over others should be self-evident. America has never been, and must never become, a theocracy, for what is religious freedom for one becomes tyranny for others.

If a person believes the earth is flat because he doesn't see any curvature while looking out over the ocean, and you tell that person that science has proven the earth is round, if he gets angry and resentful, accusing you of not being a believer, the prospect of a rational discussion dissipates.

This latter situation has become magnified over the past few years. Asking for facts is equated with challenging a person's beliefs---a dangerous thing to do these days when hatred and revenge are on the rise.

ANOTHER MASS SHOOTING. HERE'S A SUGGESTION THAT MIGHT WORK.

We will no doubt hear that familiar refrain that these mass shootings are a result of people with mental health issues who shouldn't have weapons, and that law-abiding citizens shouldn't suffer a loss of their constitutional rights because of criminals who shouldn't have guns, yet commit heinous crimes.

Two things come to mind as possible approaches.

First, although our lawmakers won't pass such a law, make parents/guardians both civilly and criminally liable for the acts of their young. The standard should be strict liability. Treat adult parents/guardians as if they committed the crimes of their children. Making adults criminally responsible--the threat of imprisonment---and civilly liable for damages--forcing them to give up their assets--might instill a sense of accountability in them. And after all, isn't personal accountability what we want for everyone?

Second, publish the names and addresses of juveniles who commit murder. Publishing the names of these killers allows the community to follow their movement and actions throughout their lives. Of course, there are those who believe juveniles shouldn't face permanent, life-altering penalties because their brains aren't fully developed. But if they commit murder and flee from police, they obviously know they did something wrong. And if they can differentiate between right and wrong, they must be held accountable and treated as adults for their crimes.

Neither one of these suggestions involve diminution of constitutional rights. Both put the blame squarely where it belongs: on the perpetrator and parents/guardians.

WHAT IS A CULT?

Donald Trump and Trumpism has been called a cult by many people, including Democratic Party leaders and even some traditional conservative Republicans who are appalled at what the party has become.

Recently, in response, some on the right wing have taken this accusation and reversed it; calling Joe Biden and the Democratic Party a cult.

Slinging accusations means nothing if there is no understanding of what the words actually mean. Therefore, it's appropriate to know what people are talking about when they exchange accusations of cultism.

A cult is "a system or group of people who practice excessive devotion to a figure, object, or belief system, typically following a charismatic leader."

Donald Trump is considered the "charismatic leader" of supporters who believe in his every word and deed. A salient feature of a cult is the members' belief in conspiracy theories, which is defined as "a belief that some covert but influential organization is responsible for a circumstance or event."

We are most familiar with QAnon, which is a "conspiracy theory originating in forum posts on the website 4chan in October 2017." Supporters believe "that Donald Trump was waging a secret war against a cabal of satanic cannibalistic pedophiles within Hollywood, the Democratic Party, and the so-called 'deep state' within the United States government. With the aid of social media platforms, the theory expanded in content and geographic reach in subsequent years and resulted in legal protests as well as several violent criminal incidents.

QAnon was the offspring of a conspiracy theory known as Pizzagate. In 2016 the website WikiLeaks released a trove of e-mails that Russian hackers had stolen from the account of John Podesta, Hillary Clinton's campaign chair for her 2016 presidential election bid. On the website 4chan—a forum characterized by trollish behaviour, extreme content, and lax moderation—anonymous users posited that the use of the term "cheese pizza" in Podesta's e-mails was code for "child pornography" and that a Washington, D.C., pizzeria named Comet Ping Pong, from which Podesta had ordered, was engaged in the sexual exploitation of children. Ultimately, Pizzagate conspiracy theorists invoked the existence of an elite cabal of satanic cannibals operating a child sex trafficking ring out of the basement of Comet Ping Pong (the restaurant does not, in fact, have a basement)." Like conspiracy theories generally, this one eventually fizzled out.

A classic example of right wing conspiracy theories is Rep. Marjorie Taylor Greene's 2018 statement that California wildfires may not have been due to climate change leaving vegetation drier and more combustible. Instead she advanced the theory that some kind of "space laser" had lit things on fire.

Recently, Greene said InfoWar's Alex Jones' vile and defamatory statements about the Sandy Hook murders as being a hoax are within his First Amendment rights, either ignorant of, or indifferent to, the fact that the freedom of speech guarantee applies to government actions, not those of private citizens. People who defame, intentionally inflict emotional distress, or cause other personal injury are responsible for them. This is known as the law of torts.

For evidence of the claims against Trump, Trumpism and his loyalists, the most glaring—although certainly not exclusive--are the following:

*Trump's repeated claims of a stolen election, despite the fact that over 60 judges who considered his claims unanimously rejected them—including judges and justices he appointed.

*The January 6 attack on the capital was not, as described by the Republican National Committee, just some overzealous Trump supporters "engaging in legitimate political discourse." The video on that day, and televised testimony of many Republicans before the House committee, readily dispose of the nonsense that is the RNC's statement. Attempts to gaslight the subject by asking Americans to believe Trump and his allies rather than what they see and hear have proven futile.

*Trump's claim that the classified records he stole from the White House belong to him and he did nothing wrong flies in the face of clearly established law that those records do not belong to Trump; they belong to the American people to be safeguarded in our national archives.

*Trump's call to Ukraine president for dirt on Hunter Biden in return for release of appropriated funds is not a "perfect" call for a president/candidate for re-election to make. The law clearly prohibits such quid pro quo behavior.

Yet, to this day, Trump continues to repeat his lies, claim he's done nothing wrong, and that he is the victim of a hoax and witch hunt. And his supporters continue to lap it up wholly without question.

As a further example of cult mentality, look at the number of Republican candidates for public office who deny the results of the 2020 presidential election, and refuse to say they will accept the outcome if they lose in November. This is directly attributable to Trump and his base.

What is critical here is the ability to distinguish fact from belief.

A fact is defined as a "thing that is known or proved to be true." In journalism, a fact is "information used as evidence or as part of a report or news article."

In law, a fact is "the truth about events as opposed to interpretation."

Facts are independently verifiable; they are established by concrete observable evidence and serve as the basis for consensus. Our tried and true methods of newsgathering, and our system of law and justice, would collapse without a foundation based on fact. Getting the facts lies at the very heart of journalism and our First Amendment freedom of the press. Our judicial system is a search for the truth by examining the facts and passing them through the law of evidence in order for them to be properly considered by judge and jury.

The four examples above about Trump are facts that have been proven to be true, used as evidence in news reports, and proven in several courts of law.

You can take those facts and place them beside the definition of a cult to see if there is any merit to calling Trump and his loyalists a cult.

Belief, however, doesn't require facts for support. It "is a state or habit of mind in which trust or confidence is placed in some person or thing."

The claim that Biden is the head of a cult is unsupported by any extrinsic fact simply because not a single fact has been offered. Unlike Trump where the evidence is observable and has passed every reasonable test, where is the evidence that Biden is head of a cult, and that his supporters are cultists? To those who offer opinion, remember that opinion is not fact. Every person is entitled to his/her opinions; they are not entitled to their facts or to supplant facts with opinion.

Biden hasn't lied about the outcome of an election, especially in the face of irrefutable fact, He hasn't stoked violence against the government, calling the attackers patriots. He hasn't stolen government records and stored them in his home. He hasn't asked a foreign government for aid against a political opponent. And there haven't been any conspiracy theories attributable to Biden like those espoused by QAnon and Taylor Greene, as well as others who sling them under the banner of the Republican Party.

Asking for facts from these accusers is a waste of time. The answer usually is something like 'It doesn't matter because you won't believe them anyway." This, of course, provides a convenient way out for avoiding the obvious: there are simply no facts supporting this wild notion.

We know that for far too many, belief is fact. It is impossible to engage in dialogue with someone who relies entirely on belief to support his/her opinions. If someone is adamant that the earth is flat, or that Biden is head of a cult, no fact will change that mindset. Facts will either be ignored, rejected or simply dismissed in words similar to those quoted in the paragraph immediately above.

All that can be done, however, is to bombard these believers with facts, facts, and more facts. Eventually, the sun will shine, the light will come on, and enlightenment will rule the day.

DOES DONALD TRUMP HAVE A MENTAL HEALTH ISSUE?

Former New Jersey Gov. Chris Christie made a fascinating assessment of Donald Trump the other days. He debunks the notion that Trump took classified records from the White House for some nefarious reason. Rather, he says, Trump more likely views those records as a trophy.

"I think it's much more likely that they're a trophy, that he walks around and says, 'Look, I've got this, I've got this classified document or that,'" Christie said. "Because, remember something, he can't believe he's not president. He can't believe he still doesn't get these documents. And he needs to display to everybody down at Mar-a-Lago, or up in Bedminster during the summer, that he still has some of those trappings."

Taking Christie's assessment to heart, CNN editor-at-large Chris Cillizza says "(Trump) has spent a lifetime playing the role of 'Donald Trump.' And his four years as president was the crowning moment in that lifetime role. He simply won't – or can't – accept that he no longer has that power and influence.

It's why he continues to push debunked election fraud conspiracies. And it's why he continues to act – for his base – like he is still president. Being able to, in the course of a conversation, to say to someone (using Christie's words) "I've got this classified document" helps preserve the illusion that Trump remains, at some level, still in power. He still (at least his own mind) has the trappings of being president, which allows him to act (and more importantly be regarded) as president."

If Christie's assessment is accurate, then he has raised a mental health issue that requires inquiry. Remember, Christie was at one time one of Trump's most ardent supporters.

Whether or not this raises a mental health issue, however, doesn't explain why so many party faithful are also election deniers; why election-denying candidates refuse to say whether they will accept the election results if they lose; and why so many believe whatever Trump says and have no difficulty with what he does.

IT'S NOT STRENGTH, IT'S WEAKNESS.

During Donald Trump's four years in the White House, he waxed often about strength and weakness. He portrayed himself as the epitome of strength, constantly pumping his clenched fist, while castigating those who disagreed with him as weak. For him, strength is power; weakness is for losers.

Yet, when he confronted Vladimir Putin in Helsinki in 2018 over Russia's claimed involvement in support of Trump during the 2016 election, Trump couldn't bend over backwards enough or use enough effusive words to praise the Russian dictator. He accepted Putin's word over the findings of his own national security officials that Trump had Russian help during his first run for the presidency.

This is not strength; it's weakness. Trump simply didn't want to offend Putin; he wanted to be his friend.

When Trump sought dirt on Hunter Biden in 2020 by asking the Ukraine president for help in return for funds, Republicans almost unanimously objected to his impeachment and conviction even though what Trump did was against the law.

This is not strength on the part of the party; it's weakness born of fear of Trump's ability to run candidates against incumbents. Remember his many calls about "primarying" those Republicans who dared to vote against him.

In the face of Trump's repeated lie that the 2020 election was stolen from him, his allies, loyalists and minions continue to deny the results, and those seeking office refuse to say whether they will accept the results if they lose.

For the election deniers and refuseniks, this is not an example of strength; it's a clear example of weakness over fear of offending Trump and his most diehard supporters.

Accepting election results lies at the heart of a democracy. Questioning them undermines public confidence in the manner by which we choose our leaders. Election denying is not strength; when done to appease one man, it's weakness.

Trump's unlawful taking of classified government records has been met by some of his most ardent cheerleaders with questions about what the FBI did or whether the public really knows what is in those documents. For them, it's not about the law that's been broken; it's about giving comfort to Trump by questioning the seizure and the contents of the records themselves. They want us to believe that he, in his own words, "did nothing wrong."

Asking the public to believe Trump did no wrong is not strength; no matter how they try to gaslight this, it's not ok to steal government records from the White House and strew them about his home. It's classic weakness born of fear of the bully.

Questioning the government's actions isn't strength; it's weakness in order to appease Trump and deflect from the lawlessness.

When Trump makes bigoted statements, his loyalists continue to refuse to hold his hand to the fire by failing to roundly condemn such atrocious behavior from someone who held the highest office in the land. This is weakness again born of fear of antagonizing him.

When Trump proceeds with his pity party, enraging his minions with self-serving claims of victimization, they lap up his "poor, poor, pity me" railings with blind acceptance, manifested by loud cheers and wild applause.

This is not strength; it's weakness; weakness in not being strong enough to stand up to the lies, lawlessness and vile, offensive language of the party's leader.

To be sure, there are other examples of weakness in not challenging Trump's words or deeds. The examples here, however, make the point.

As for Trump, strength is not to be equated with vile language or lawless actions.

No matter how hard they try to portray strength, those Republican Party members who fail or refuse to call out Trump for his deviant actions are weak.

WHY?

There are eight overarching principles that represent the conservative approach to government. For each one, it is important that the public ask those who preach them WHY? when their words are matched against their deeds.

Individual Freedom. If Republicans truly support individual freedom, why do they approve of the government telling a woman what she can and can't do with her body? Why do they approve the government telling teachers what they can and can't teach; students what they can and can't study; businesses what they can and can't say about government practices; universities and colleges what they can and can't teach; college students what they can and can't say or learn? If parents are to be empowered to make decisions for their children, why does the Republican Party take it upon itself to decide what books to ban? These forms of government-imposed restrictions on freedom based on ideological fixation make a mockery of their limited government stance. Those who are restricted by these government actions don't have the individual freedom Republicans promise.

Family Values. If Republicans truly believe in family values, including abortion as murder, why do so many still support Georgia senate candidate Herschel Walker? He has denied he paid a woman to have an abortion, yet admits to giving her $700 without saying why he did this. Walker's denials, after so many lies causing him to backtrack, don't pass the smell test. For the Republican Party, taking control of the Senate is more important than being faithful to their self-serving family values claim.

Further, what does it say about Republicans on this point when they support Walker's conduct—as well as that of Donald Trump and his litany of potential criminal activities stretching from January 6 to those government records found strewn through his estate? Their railings against Hunter Biden and other enemies while remaining either supportive or silent on the facts of Trump's conduct and those of some of his allies make a mockery of their family values claim.

Limited Government. How can Republicans favor limited government when they impose their ideology on others through multiple government actions? See the points made under their Individual Freedom claim. Further, some leading Republicans have made it their mission to place the primacy of the Christian religion in government. This is not limited government; it's the promise of theocracy where one religion superintends government. Actions do speak louder than words.

The Rule of Law. Repeated election lies, election denials, refusing to accept election results, stealing government records, subpoena snubs, pardon pleas, threatening violence if criminal charges are filed, etc. The rule of law is accepting the results of an election. The rule of law is not undermining the nation's democratic election process. In the face of these actions, therefore, how can the Republicans' legitimately lay claim to the high ground of the rule of law?

Peace Through Strength. If Republicans truly believe this, why do so many support Russian despot Vladimir Putin in his war against Ukraine, and his verbal assault against our nation's most important allies in NATO? Supporting a war monger who attacks a smaller nation is not an example of peace through strength; it's another example of placating and appeasing Putin, not unlike what Trump did in Helsinki in 2018 over reports of Russia helping Trump in the 2016 election. Trump rejected his own national security team in favor of Putin's bland denial.

Fiscal Responsibility. If Republicans truly believe in fiscal responsibility through less taxes, why do they insist on permanent tax breaks for the wealthy, but only temporary tax relief for the middle class on down? And why do they provide tax benefits and other economic advantages for the wealthy, yet oppose any program that provides economic benefits to others? These tax breaks are a form of corporate welfare; for Republicans, that's ok. It's economic benefits for those people in demonstrable need that gets their goat.

And why do they insist on undermine two pillars of our economic foundation, Social Security and Medicare, not by strengthening them, but by sunsetting them and subjecting them to re-enactment by a conservative Congress that has historically shown disfavor for both programs? Haven't Republicans considered the economic impact of the nation should both of these programs be scrapped? Perhaps they have, and simply don't care.

Free Markets. We know that Republicans believe in businesses operating without restriction; that is, unfettered markets. They have also talked about privatizing Social Security and Medicare, as well as other federal programs that they don't like, regardless of the fact that they benefit a majority of Americans. History, however, instructs most glaringly what happens when businesses run amok without government oversight. We need only look to the Great Depression of 1929 and the Great Meltdown of 2008. What guarantees will the Republicans provide to assure that their business model doesn't lead to economic conflagrations like these two? So far, silence on that subject.

Human Dignity. For their final point, Republicans claim to favor human dignity. Frankly, I don't know of any politician who doesn't favor human dignity. But since the Republicans claim the high road here as well, it's appropriate to ask how the party shows human dignity by restricting the words and actions of those persons referenced in the other seven categories. Women, educators, students, businesses who refuse to kowtow to the party line, etc. How is human dignity fostered by ending or turning over Social Security and Medicare to the whims (and greed) of the big corporations?

The next time you hear a Republican Party official wax on what the party stands for, ask yourself how what they say squares with what they do, or promise to do.

Echoing another favorite party line, hold them accountable to make sure their deeds match their words.

TIME TO GET OFF THE TRUMP TRAIN?

A federal judge is the latest to expose the irrefutable fact that Donald Trump knew his election fraud claims were false. The judge, in reviewing email exchanges, issued his ruling that some email must be turned over the House committee investigating the January 6 attack on the capital because they are not protected by executive privilege; rather, they are clear evidence of criminal conduct that is not protected by that privilege.

Irrefutable evidence of Trump's knowingly false claims poured forth from several Republicans who testified during the committee's televised hearings held over the summer. That attack resulted in several deaths and many injuries, including law enforcement officers.

It's never easy for people who believed so strongly in someone that they've been conned by a master con artist and manipulator.

Trump's defense is the same as it has been from the beginning: it's all a hoax, witch hunt, yada, yada, yada. Not a single word is uttered under oath, unlike those who testified before the committee.

Trump won't testify under oath because he risks having to tell the truth or face perjury charges. So long as he believes he has millions of supporters who believe his lies, he'll continue to press them even as evidence continues to mount against him.

His psyche doesn't allow him to admit publicly that he lied, and that his lies pose a clear and present danger to our Democracy.

Trump's deviant conduct over the years is now in the public domain. The number of investigations, lawsuits covering his pre-presidential, presidential, and post-presidential years (stolen government records being the most prominent of the latter) are all out in the open, awareness growing by leaps and bounds with each passing day.

With all of this information out there, the question that naturally arises is what will it take for Trump's most ardent loyalists, his MAGA minions, to admit to themselves that they've been conned? For them, when is enough enough?

A collateral question is what will it take for those public officials who continue to back him out of fear of by primaried, to say it's time to get off the Trump train? What will it take for them to say enough is enough?

To this day, the election deniers and results refuseniks persist even as the evidence of the magnitude of Trump's lies continue to pour out. What will it take for them to show some courage and some spine to say "enough is enough?"

There are certainly other Republican candidates out there whose bandwagons the MAGA folks could easily join; those who blindly believe Trump represents true Republican values.

Why do they continue to stay on the Trump train as it barrels onward toward the abyss?

ARE THERE BOTH SIDES TO ALL ISSUES? I HOPE NOT.

Recently, I saw an ad on NewsNation in which a conservative offers praise for the network in presenting both sides of the issues in a fair and balanced manner.

This brought to mind the many times conservatives railed against the mainstream media for failing to present both sides of issues of public importance. This is premised on their belief that only the liberal side is presented, and that the conservative viewpoint is being ignored or silenced.

But aren't there some issues for which there is only one side—the side that supports a democracy? As you consider the list below, ask what the conservative viewpoint is for each question.

What are the two sides when it comes to white supremacy?

What are the two sides when it comes to neo-Naziism? Reflect on former President Trump's 2018 statement that "there are some very fine people" who are white nationalists/neo-Nazis.

What are the two sides when it comes to some conservative claims that the Christian religion should be directing the government?

What are the two sides when it comes to government banning books based on specific content and viewpoint the government doesn't like?

What are the two sides when it comes to government control over what can and can't be taught in colleges and universities, and public and private schools?

What are the two sides when it comes to conservative support for Vladimir Putin in his war against Ukraine and his attack on our NATO allies?

What are the two sides when it comes to denying election results despite all of the facts to the contrary?

What are the two sides when it comes to accepting the results of an election, knowing that to do otherwise undermines the process that lies at the heart of our Democracy?

What are the two sides when it comes to honoring a subpoena duly issued by a lawful authority?

What are the two sides in assuring the preservation of Social Security and Medicare?

There is no doubt that there are other issues that compel a loud, unified voice; these ten, however, should suffice in gleaning what is the conservative position.

Do conservatives support the goals of white supremacists? Do they favor white nationalists/neo-Nazis? Do they support the Christian religion directing our government? Do they favor government banning books, or controlling school curriculum and instruction based on particular viewpoint? Do they support Putin in his war against Ukraine, and his attacks on NATO? Do they endorse election deniers and those who refuse to accept election results unless they win? Do they support those who reject the authority of subpoenas as an integral part of our judicial system? Do they support plans to sunset or privatize Social Security and Medicare?

Let's see if conservatives take up the challenge and say what they really stand for.

Cut the "Socialism" and "radical left-wing cult" and other language designed to anger, and provide straight answers to these questions. Then, by comparing answers to what they preach, we can clearly see whether conservatives are really for individual freedom, limited government, the rule of law, peace through strength, human dignity, etc., etc., etc.

We get a lot of angry, threatening rhetoric from the Republican Party. Let's see if we can get some clear answers.

"GETTING OLD ISN'T FOR SISSIES."

This take on a line from screen legend Bette Davis just about sums up where I am today. Yesterday, I visited one of my orthopedic doctors (yes, I've had several over the years) for injections to ease my low back pain. To echo the words from Alcoholics Anonymous, "I am an Arthritic."

Now, lots of folks have arthritis, especially those of us who have reached senior citizen status. But some have more arthritis than others. That's me. Lucky me.

I figure my parents had a choice: they could have left me with their millions, or their osteoarthritic conditions. Well, they really didn't have a choice; since they didn't have millions. So, they left me with the only other thing they both had--a lifetime of these memories that I would gladly sell if I had two things, the ability to sell and a willing masochistic buyer. Well, it is an inheritance, isn't it?

As a child, I remember asking my dad why he was so stooped over. He told me what his mom told him when he asked her: "Well, that's where the money is." Dad said you'll have a far better chance finding that dollar bill on the ground than standing straight up. Of course, stooped shoulders is a product of age; when arthritis is added to the mix, well, you get the picture. When the pain increases, I find myself stooped over, spending more and more time looking at the ground. I've actually picked up a few pennies, nickels, dimes and quarters over the years, and there was that $20 bill I found in a parking lot, so my grandma certainly spoke words of great wisdom.

My first introduction to arthritis was when I was 38. I was shaving one morning and, as I tried to stand up from leaning over the sink, got this sharp, stabbing pain in my lower back. An emergency visit to my first orthopedist and a few days of ice and naproxen eased the pain. (These days, when

I take Aleve, I remind myself that I took both naproxen and ibuprofen when they were prescription medications. In fact, over the years, I've had prescribed just about every pain pill and NSAIDs on the market.)

Since then, I've had five knee surgeries, both knees replaced, right shoulder replaced, eight other shoulder surgeries, several surgeries for trigger fingers, both thumbs rebuilt—more than two dozen orthopedic surgeries by eight different doctors.

I also had seven vertebrae in my neck and upper back fused so that I no longer have lateral head movement. This resulted from a condition called Forestier's disease. Picture your spine as a candelabra. Now, picture hot, dripping wax pouring over that candelabra. That was the condition of my spine 12 years ago. My spine was deteriorating, and would have fused automatically over a few years—an extremely painful few years. So, it was a choice of immediate fusion or years of intense pain. Great choice, eh? To this day, I live with neck pain for which I see a neurologist who injects Botox into my neck four times each year to ease the pain.

I am jokingly called the Bionic Man by the wonderful folks at the Tallahassee Orthopedic Center. Personally, I think I deserve a wing bearing my name.

I think that when we reach a certain age, all of us have to visit an "ist" of one kind or another. Oncologist, rheumatologist, cardiologist, you get the point. Well, for me, I suppose I'm very lucky: I have only two "ists" that I see regularly, the orthopedist who is a pain management physician who handles, well, pain management, and the neurologist for Botox injections. Lots of needles. (There's also a urologist that I see for annual checkups, and my primary physician who makes sure all systems are functioning properly—or at least as properly as they can as I near 80, but that's it.)

The key here is that it's all about pain management. I'll never be free of pain; that's the toll arthritis takes. However, the degree of pain can be managed. I get inflammatory flareups. When they hit, the pain increases. As I get older, these flareups become more frequent, more intense and last longer.

The key to dealing with arthritis pain is to keep moving. Even when the pain is great, movement is essential, otherwise there is great risk in a downward cycle of the joint freezing into its continually deteriorating position. But when exercise, physical therapy and medication no longer ease the pain, and surgery can't be performed when there is significant arthritis (as in my lower back), injections are what's left in the physician's tool bag. And movement even when you don't want to do anything. For me, it's a three-mile walk at a moderate pace every other day at the Premier track, and one hour of aerobic exercises in the pool in between. These exercises actually do reduce the pain level, albeit temporarily.

I get upset when I read directions on OTC medications: "For temporary relief." Who the hell wants only temporary relief? I look for the day when medicine announces a pain pill that is advertised as "For permanent relief." Yeah, right.

I guess I should consider myself lucky that I'm not a patient for those doctors who treat the serious stuff, but there are days......

Next up for me is what the orthopedists call radiofrequency ablation, or rhizotomy. In laymen's terms, this involves use of a needle to kill nerve ends, those pesky pain transmitters that cause so much trouble. I had this procedure over 10 years ago and it worked. There's every reason it will work again, hopefully for 10 more years. Then I can look forward to this helpful procedure every 10 years. Now that's optimism.

After I had my neck fused and faced a couple of years of recovery, I took Neil Sedaka's great song "Breaking Up is Hard to Do," and wrote a parody. I'll end this note for those who are musically inclined (and those who aren't) with my feelings back then:

(Chorus: Down doo-be-doo fall down, a downa downa down doo-be-doo fall down, a downa downa down doo-be-doo fall down, getting old is hard to do.)

Please take these pains away from me

Arthritis leaves me in misery

All these aches just make me blue

Getting old is hard to do.

Years ago, I had no pain,

Now I think it's just so insane

After all that I go through

Yes, getting old is hard to do,

I said that getting old is hard to do

Hard to hear, and hard to chew

Don't say that this is my fate

Don't tell me getting old is really all that great

I won't give in, I'm a stubborn guy

No need to give a reason why

Joint replacement and orthopedic shoes

Yes, getting old is hard to do.

OK, it's not Johnny Mercer, Cole Porter, Carole King, or even Bud Abbott and Lou Costello. (Actually, considering what passes for good lyrics these days, perhaps my effort isn't so bad.)

But all things considered--my family, my friends, my career, things I've done, I'll take the arthritis if I must. I'll just manage it to the best of my ability, do the best I can each day, and keep my eyes on the future.

In the immortal words of Yankee great Lou Gehrig, "I consider myself the luckiest man on the face of the earth."

ON THE REPUBLICANS' THREAT TO IMPEACH JOE BIDEN, MERRICK GARLAND AND CHRISTOPHER WRAY—AND ANYONE ELSE.

As Republicans stand at the cusp of gaining control of Congress—or at least the House of Representatives—they are sharpening their knives in anticipation of carrying out threats to impeach President Biden, Attorney General Garland and FBI Director Wray—and possibly others who stand in their way.

Impeachment talk about Biden is in revenge for the House impeachments of Donald Trump. Some of the grounds mentioned include the Afghanistan withdrawal, failure to secure the nation's southern border, and whatever they hope to find that connects father with son Hunter Biden.

For Garland and Wray, the threat of impeachment centers around the raid conducted at Trump's Mar-a-Lago estate leading to the seizure of highly classified and other government records taken from the White House in violation of federal law.

The Constitution provides that a president (as well as other federal officials) may be impeached only upon the grounds of "high crimes and misdemeanors." Interestingly, this term has never been defined or its parameters set by the United States Supreme Court.

In the past, the Court has refused to address actions taken wholly within the jurisdiction of another branch of government. In other words, and by example, the Court won't superintend a president's decision to issue a pardon because that decision is solely and exclusively within the jurisdiction of the president.

Here's the rub, however. Biden's Afghanistan withdrawal was purely a policy decision. Pointedly, there's been no allegation that a law was broken, or that Biden violated his oath of office or the public trust.

The raid at Mar-a-Lago was conducted in strict accordance with the law—the issuance of a subpoena by a federal judge based on a showing of probable cause. Again, there's been no allegation that a law was broken, or that either Garland or Wray violated their oaths or the public trust.

Biden, in response to Republican leaders' threats to pass whatever they want and force a government shutdown to get their way, has threatened to veto every piece of legislation they send to him that, in his view, threatens our Democracy and undermines our nation's guiding principles.

This raises the specter of whether policy decisions and legislative vetoes will be converted by the Republicans to "high crimes and misdemeanors." The prospect of converting the rarely used power of impeachment into a weapon by one party to weaken the authority of a president of the opposite party should send shock waves through those who value our Democracy. Yet, it is a real possibility that, if the Republicans carry through on their threat, the Democrats could well do likewise the next time they control at least the House of Representatives with a Republican in the White House. This tit-for-tat use of the constitutional power of impeachment is not what our Founding Fathers envisioned for our emerging nation.

Of course, Republicans will never get the required 2/3 vote to convict and remove Biden, Garland or Wray, but that doesn't matter; it's the show of support for Trump and his MAGAites that counts. For them, revenge matters.

Even though the Supreme Court majority is firmly in the hands of the conservative wing, protecting the institution of the Court itself might compel the justices to chime in on the parameters of "high crimes and misdemeanors" if the need arises.

Former President Gerald Ford offered a famous, and flip, definition of that phrase: "An impeachable offense is whatever a majority of the House of Representatives considers it to be at a given moment in history."

Assuming this is correct, could the House impeach a president for not appointing people Republicans want? How about a decision to enforce a law not to the liking of the House Republicans? What about not ordering an investigation into someone the House wants investigated, or ordering an investigation into someone the House doesn't want investigated? In fact, how about any policy decision or executive order the opposing party doesn't like?

I could go on and on with examples of decisions wholly within the domain of the president and his appointees, but you get the point. Impeachment based on revenge or likes and dislikes places the issue squarely where it legitimately belongs: on the Supreme Court.

In 1803, the United States Supreme Court in <u>Marbury v. Madison,</u> firmly established that the Court has the power to determine the constitutionality and validity of the acts of the other two branches of government – a concept that is a fundamental characteristic of American government. From this, the constitutionality of a House determination of "high crimes and misdemeanors" is clearly within the Court's jurisdiction. The critical point here is the impeachment is an exercise by the legislative branch against officials in the executive and judicial branches of government. This inter-branch relationship compels the Court to settle their disputes.

Legal scholars scoff at Ford's definition and note that impeachment doesn't necessarily depend on the commission of a crime.

Frank Bowman, a law professor at the University of Missouri School of Law and the author of *High Crimes & Misdemeanors: A History of Impeachment for the Age of Trump*, believes it doesn't. "The defenders of the impeached officer always argue, always, that a crime is required," he says. "And every time that misconception has to be knocked down again."

He offers this example: "Let's say the President were to wake up tomorrow morning and says, 'All this impeachment stuff is kind of getting on my nerves. I think I'm going to go to Barbados for six months. Don't call me, I'll call you,' and just cuts off all contact and refuses to do his duty," Bowman theorizes. "That's not a crime. It's not violating a law. But could we impeach him? Of course we could — otherwise what's the remedy? We have a country without a President." (As a note, this could be viewed as abandonment of office, nonfeasance, misfeasance or malfeasance, dereliction of duty, violating the oath of office to "take care that the laws be faithfully executed," violation of the public trust, etc.)

To understand what the framers thought "high crimes and misdemeanors" meant, Harvard Law professor Jennifer Taub points to Alexander Hamilton's Federalist Paper No. 65, in which he explains the impeachment process. "The subjects of its jurisdiction are those offenses which proceed from the misconduct of public men, or, in other words, from the abuse or violation of some public trust," Hamilton wrote in 1788.

The first person who was successfully impeached and removed was federal judge John Pickering in 1803. He was impeached because, as the University of Missouri's Bowman says, "He was both an alcoholic and probably insane." Bowman points out that neither was a crime, but led him to abuse his office.

Only 20 people were impeached in the U.S. from 1788 through Donald Trump: three Presidents, one Senator, one Secretary of War and 15 federal judges.

If a Republican-controlled House of Representatives follows through on its impeachment promises, compare whatever charges they bring forth with those charges against the 20 who were charged previously. This subject is too important to ignore or leave to the judgment of revenge-seekers. We are, after all, talking about our most sacred document—our Constitution. A brief history of impeachment follows.

Andrew Johnson was the first president to be impeached. Nine of the eleven articles of impeachment against him related to violating the Tenure of Office Act. which contained a provision making a violation a high crime and misdemeanor. He was acquitted of removing Secretary of War Edwin Stanton from office. However, this impeachment was in the context of a deep disagreement between Johnson and Congress about reconstruction after the Civil War.

President Bill Clinton was impeached in 1998 on two counts of "high crimes and misdemeanors": lying under oath to a federal grand jury and obstruction of justice. The charges emerged after Clinton denied having had a sexual relationship with White House intern Monica Lewinsky in the course of a civil sexual harassment lawsuit against Clinton by Paula Jones. He was acquitted by the Senate.

President Donald Trump was first impeached for abuse of power and obstruction of justice when evidence was produced indicating that he tried to use foreign policy toward Ukraine for personal political gain. His second impeachment was on the charge of incitement of insurrection when Trump supporters, acting on his false election conspiracy theories, launched an at the Capitol, and Trump dithered in response to it.

Sen. William Blount of Tennessee was impeached in 1797 for conspiring to assist in Great Britain's attempt to Spanish-controlled territories in modern-day Florida and Louisiana. (Expelled before trial.)

Secretary of War William W. Belknap was impeached in 1876 for criminal disregard for his office and accepting payments in exchange for making appointments. (Acquitted).

Associate Supreme Court Justice Samuel Chase was impeached in 1804 for arbitrary and oppressive conduct of trials. (Acquitted.)

Associate Judge of the Commerce Court Robert W. Archbald was impeached for improper business relations with clients. (Removed from office.)

Thirteen federal district judges were impeached for are variety of reasons:

intoxication on the bench and unlawful handling of property claims (John Pickering 1803—removed); abuse of contempt power (James H. Peck 1830—acquitted); refusing to hold court and waging war against the United States (West H. Humphreys 1862—removed); intoxication on the bench (Mark Delahay 1873—resigned before trial); abuse of contempt power and other abuses of office (Charles Swayze 1912—removed); abuse of power (George W. English 1926—resigned before trial); favoritism in appointment of bankruptcy receivers (Harold Louderback 1933—acquitted); favoritism in appointing bankruptcy receivers and practicing law as a sitting judge (Halsted Ritter 1936—removed from office); income tax evasion and remaining as judge following criminal conviction (Harry Claiborne 1986—removed from office); perjury and conspiracy to solicit a bribe (Alcee Hastings 1988—removed from office); perjury before a federal grand jury (Walter Nixon 1989—removed from office); sexual assault, obstructing and impeding an official proceeding, and making false and misleading statements (Samuel B. Kent 2009—resigned); and accepting bribes and making false statements under oath (G. Thomas Porteous, Jr. 2010—removed from office).

IT'S TIME FOR THAT "COMMON GROUND" DISCUSSION, BUT FIRST....

As the November midterm elections draw near and the rhetoric between liberals and conservatives ratchets up, it's important that we all realize that we live in one country united under one national constitution and one form of government that has sustained us for almost 250 years.

As anger rages and fingers are pointed, soon now, this election cycle will be history, and we will have to live with the results.

We might as well try to talk to one another than continue this dangerous spiral of heated rhetoric, anger, resentment, casting blame, and violence.

To put it directly, we need to heed those calls for finding common ground. We need those common ground discussions going forward. Before that can happen, though, we need to be sure we're talking about facts, not beliefs.

Beliefs are personal; they don't necessarily have to be based on fact. Common ground, however, requires a foundation upon which we can all agree. That foundation is one of fact; identifiable, verifiable fact.

For example, our system of justice is based on a search for the truth, which is a search for facts. We expect law enforcement officials to conduct investigations and reach their conclusions based on fact. A person can't be legally arrested and charged based on belief, and a prosecutor can't do his or her job based on belief. A jury can't convict anyone simply because the jurors believe someone to be guilty. And a judge can't send anyone to jail based on his or her belief.

Similarly, we rely on the media to give us the facts so that we may be properly informed, allowing us to draw reasonable, logical conclusions.

Sadly and regrettably, over the past few years dangerous conspiratorial theories have garnered much of the media's attention, and far too many Americans have taken those theories to heart and to this day, believe at least some to be true.

In order to be faithful in the search for common ground, however, some of those wilder theories—including those that have been debunked but still believed by many, must be categorically rejected. Below is a list of conspiracy theories reversed and placed in their factual context.

Accepting these statements as facts will go a long way toward finding common ground.

*Democrats were not running a child pedophile operation in the basement of a pizza parlor in Washington, D. C.

*Donald Trump lost the 2020 election fair and square, not as the result of a rigged election.

*California forest fires were not caused by shooting laser beams at the trees.

*The Democratic Party is not a Satanic cult engaging in devil worship.

*There is no such thing as a vast global network that tortures and sexually abuses children in Satanic rituals.

*Donald Trump wasn't—and isn't---secretly preparing a mass arrest of government officials and celebrities.

*Celebrities are not harvesting adrenochrome from children's bodies.

*Robert Mueller was not investigating a child-sex trafficking network.

*There is no link between vaccines and autism.

*COVID-19 vaccines haven't had, and won't have, tracking chips activated by 5G networks.

*COVID wasn't, isn't, a hoax.

*COVID-19 was not created in a lab in China.

*Climate change is real, and humans play a significant role in climate change.

*Several mass shootings in recent years were not staged hoaxes.

*Barack Obama was born in the United States.

*Humans landed on the moon in the late 60s and 70s.

*The September 11th attacks on the World Trade Center and Pentagon were carried out by 19 terrorists supported by Al-Qaeda.

*Donald Trump's call to Ukraine president for dirt on Hunter Biden in exchange for funds was against the law.

*Donald Trump instigated an attack on the Capitol on January 6.

*The FBI raid on Donald Trump's estate was carried out under a probable cause warrant lawfully issued by a federal judge.

In an attempt to reach common ground, here are some of the things Democrats support. Gage your reaction to each as you frame your approach toward that common ground.

Democrats favor social programs, labor unions, consumer protection, workplace safety regulation, equal opportunity, disability rights, racial equity, regulations against environmental pollution, and criminal justice reform. Democrats tend to support abortion rights and the LGBT community, as well as a pathway to citizenship for undocumented immigrants. Democrats typically agree with the scientific consensus on climate change and favor a multilateral approach in foreign policy.

Democrats support Social Security and Medicare, and favor secure pension programs that provide a guaranteed financial foundation in retirement. They oppose privatizing these bedrock sources of that foundation because of the vagaries of a free market, such as what took place during the Great Recession of 2008.

THE RAGING DEBATE OVER THE RULE OF LAW AND REQUIRING TOP GOVERNMENT OFFICIALS TO TESTIFY UNDER OATH.

There is a well-known principle of law that the public is entitled to every man's evidence.

Tell that to Donald Trump, who continues to rely on executive privilege to avoid testifying under oath and offering evidence on potential criminal activity.

Tell that to Lindsey Graham, who's relying on the Constitution's speech and debate clause to avoid testifying under oath about his calls to Georgia officials following the 2020 presidential election. Those officials want to see if any skullduggery was involved.

And tell that to Florida Gov. Ron DeSantis, who is relying on the apex doctrine's prohibition against requiring a top government official to testify under oath if he lacks personal knowledge and there are other sources available who have the sought-after information. Similarly, the purpose of this inquiry is to see if there was any skullduggery involved.

In each case, what is sought by investigators is not information regarding legitimate official government action; rather, what is sought is whether there was criminal activity or other nefarious skullduggery involved that isn't protected by a privilege.

There is a continuing, raging debate between Democrats and Republicans over what the oft-repeated phrase "rule of law" really means. Republicans like to conflate this with "law and order," hoping voters will think about street crime in states and cities run by Democrats. In turn, Democrats typically point to the high crime rates in states and cities run by Republicans, while also focusing on crimes in the White House under Donald Trump, and crimes possibly committed by his supporters in Congress.

There is a well-known principle of law that is tied to the rule of law; the United States Supreme Court has repeatedly said: "In its pursuit of truth and justice, the American judicial system has long relied on the principle that the public 'has a right to every man's evidence.' To this end, courts rely on a strong presumption against recognizing evidentiary privileges."

It is the application of these privileges that lie at the heart of the search for the truth. It's important to compare this principle with the reality of its application to top government officials. The following description of privileges proves that the public doesn't always have the right to every person's evidence.

We are familiar with former President Trump's efforts to avoid testifying under oath, relying on the doctrine of executive privilege. This doctrine defines the authority of the president to withhold documents or information in his possession or in the possession of the executive branch from the legislative or judicial branch of the government. Several of Trump's former staffers have also relied on executive privilege in refusing to disclose information under oath to Congress and the courts.

The latest example of the application of a doctrine that prohibits fact-gathering inquiry is the one relied on by Sen. Lindsey Graham. Graham has been subpoenaed to testify in connection with his post-2020 election conversations with Georgia officials. At the time of his calls to Georgia, Trump was asking those same officials to find enough votes to secure Georgia's electoral college vote.

Graham, relying on the Constitution's speech and debate clause, maintains he is absolutely immune from having to testify. He argues that his calls were part of his "legislative fact-finding" mission and therefore the Constitution insulates him from such subpoena demands. The debate clause shields legislators from certain law enforcement activities when participating in legislative duties. However, it doesn't shield inquiry into matters that are distinct from legislative duties, like helping out Trump in securing electoral college votes.

Georgia officials maintain Graham was acting in concert with Trump in the ex-president's efforts to seek electoral assistance. Both the federal district and appeals courts backed Georgia's position; however, the Supreme Court, through Justice Thomas (a staunch Trump supporter), blocked the lower courts' rulings until the full Court considers Graham's claims.

As Graham tries to shield himself behind the speech and debate clause, another public official is relying on yet another doctrine to shield himself from having to testify under oath.

Florida Gov. Ron DeSantis is relying on the "apex doctrine" in trying to avoid testifying about his efforts to have the state legislature enact a congressional redistricting plan that skewers several former districts that favored African-American voters and representatives.

This doctrine, expressly adopted in some jurisdictions including Florida, protects the top officers of government from being deposed without a showing that they have unique or special knowledge of the events in question, and that the party seeking the deposition is unable to obtain the information using other sources.

In short, for the governor to rely on the apex doctrine, he must show that (1) he lacks unique, first-hand knowledge of the facts at issue and (2) other, less intrusive means of discovery have not been exhausted. DeSantis' problem in relying on this defense is that he was personally involved in preparing the congressional redistricting plan that he cajoled the legislature to pass. How he overcomes the two points noted above will make for interesting court sessions.

There are other doctrines that impact an official's requirement to testify and implicate entitlement to every man's evidence.

Legislators are precluded from being compelled to testify regarding legislative matters. Legislators generally speak through the legislation they pass. There are rules of statutory construction that permit parties to argue over, and judges to interpret, what a statute means; therefore, asking a legislator why he or she voted, or failed to vote, on a particular bill, or what were his motives in connection with legislation, is off-limits.

Members of the executive branch are precluded from testifying on matters of policy as well as any matter that is covered by the powers and duties of that branch of government.

A judge is immune from having to testify as to his or her mental impressions. A judge speaks through opinions, judgments and orders. It is improper to question a judge as to why he or she ruled a certain way, took any action that might involve judicial inquiry, or on any matter within the exercise of the judge's jurisdiction.

Similarly, prosecutors can't be compelled to testify regarding prosecutorial decisions. Why he or she decides to prosecute; witnesses to be called; etc., or any matter that impacts the prosecutors' official duties and actions are off-limits.

There is also the attorney-client privilege. This has been asserted along with executive privilege where officials additionally claim they had discussions with legal counsel. This privilege is the legal protection from discovery or disclosure of specific evidence or information related to a legal matter.

These privileges serve a useful purpose in having officials avoid harassment and burdensome or annoying baseless litigation, while protecting important communications requiring free exchange of ideas, etc. But when used as a shield to prevent inquiry into criminal or other aberrant conduct, the courts will prevent an abuse of privilege.

The tension between those who assert a privilege and those who want evidence usually focuses on whether there is potential criminal or other aberrant behavior involved. Government officials cannot hide that behind a privilege.

MICROPHONITIS

Once again, we bear witness to the miracles of modern science and medicine. A disease that affects many politicians has just been finally identified. It's called Microphonitis.

We have all seen this affliction on display. Intelligent, experienced politicians who would never say silly, asinine, dumb or weird things suddenly blurt them out when standing before this metallic object which they know amplifies their voices to the mass audience.

So, instead of sounding like they deserve to hold public office, they sound like they've been schooled by the Three Stooges.

Until this medical breakthrough, a politician's incredible statements were brushed off as gaffes. A gaffe is an unintentional act or remark causing embarrassment to the speaker. Joe Biden, in his more than 40 years in public office, is a gaffe machine. He's smart, well educated, and well-versed in politics; but when he gets in front of a microphone, he's bound to say something that's gaffey (rhymes with daffy).

But we now know that simply dismissing such cuckoo comments as gaffes doesn't explain why they happen. Microphonitis offers that explanation.

Three prefatory notes here.

First, it seems that Microphonitis affects only those who have a demonstrable IQ that is at least one point above stupid. The scientific explanation behind this is that stupid people believe that everything they say is intelligent and imbued with wisdom. They believe this because they are incapable of distinguishing between smart and stupid. For them, everything they say is smart; for the rest, what they say is stupid. But since we don't know the actual IQ of many of these people, we have to assume these folks are smart enough to suffer from Microphonitis.

Second, this affliction also hits those who aren't politicians, but think they are. The latest example here is Ye, who used to be Kanye West until he decided to shorten it, perhaps because his adoring public had difficulty spelling Kanye. In any event, he made some outrageous anti-Semitic statements, for which several of his endorsing companies have dropped him like a bad habit. Now, it may be that his IQ doesn't rise to the level where he can be excused for not knowing the difference between smart and stupid, but we must give him the benefit of the doubt, which may be removed if he continues to make outrageous statements. Thus, it's that dadgum microphonitis. Either that, or, in the immortal words of Forrest Gump, stupid is as stupid does.

Third, Microphonitis doesn't seem to affect those who follow a prepared script and don't go off ad-libbing. Once they want to show how smart they are and depart from the script, you can bet the mortgage that very soon thereafter, you will hear the effects of this disease, which by the way seems more rampant in Washington, D.C. and state capital cities.

So, what is the scientific explanation behind Microphonitis? Glad you asked. Well, it seems that when a politician sees a microphone before him/her, 10 percent of the cells located in the thinking part of the brain suddenly begin to collide with each other. Half of them are excited to be able to speak to an audience; the other half is thinking about what should or shouldn't be said. These two factions of cells, each seeking the upper hand, start warring with each other. It is this brain battle that causes these momentary slipups we formerly called gaffes, but can now be readily identified as the harmful effects of Microphonitis.

The latest recorded example was just the other day, when House Speaker Nancy Pelosi said the upcoming election isn't really about inflation, but about the cost of living in America. Huh? I thought inflation is the cost of living, but in any event, you see how a skilled politician can easily fall victim to Microphonitis.

During his turbulent four-year term as president, Donald Trump made embarrassing statements. Lots of them. Remember his suggestion that ingesting bleach might cure COVID? A listing of his gaffes would fill a book. But we now know precisely why he said wild and crazy things. Note that he didn't make these goofy statements during his television show because that was carefully scripted. But once he became a politician and a microphone was placed before him, necessitating him to speak without a script, well, you know what I'm referring to.

I could provide a long list of victims of this affliction. Marjorie Taylor Greene and Lauren Boebert come to mind, but there are certainly many others who utter crazy things on a daily basis. Each is presumed to be inflicted with Microphonitis.

The cure, of course, should be obvious: just keep these folks away from a microphone. Either that, or make every statement from a carefully prepared script—and don't go off showing how smart they are by ad-libbing or going off script.

And remember that this breakthrough doesn't apply to the genuinely stupid. Re-read my first prefatory note. Recall Forrest Gump's statement. And finally, remember this: you can't fix stupid.

So there you have it. The next time you hear a crazy comment, it's a result of Microphonitis. Or stupidity.

PENCE ADVOCATES RELIGIOUS INTOLERANCE.

Former Vice President Mike Pence told FOX News the First Amendment to the United States Constitution does not protect Americans from having other people's faiths forced upon them. He also suggested that the Supreme Court's right-wing supermajority has a duty to side with one faith over others. Today, that means the GOP's embrace of Christian nationalism.

My understanding of early American history is that the Pilgrims and Puritans came to America from England to escape religious persecution and practice religious freedom. The ability to practice one's religious beliefs free from government interference lies at the heart of the First Amendment.

But Pence and his true believers would turn the freedom from compelled religion on its ear. That one group's religious doctrine can be given national prominence over all others, and that group's beliefs can be forced on others— even to the point of persecuting those who refuse to accept another's dogma---should send shock waves through those who understand our nation's history of religious tolerance that underpins our First Amendment. Whether it's indifference to, or ignorance of, our nation's history, what Pence advocates should be summarily rejected by those who understand the history of religious freedom in America.

Religion is an intensely personal matter. Each of us has the right to practice his/her religious beliefs free from government preference or interference. In truth, government must not take sides; it must act to assure that religion in America is practiced in complete freedom. The kind of mentality demonstrated by Pence and his fellow believers must never see the light of day in America.

THE TIME-WORN ISSUES AGAIN: THE ECONOMY AND CRIME. THE CURE COULD BE WORSE THAN THE ILLNESS.

As we move toward the November midterm elections, two issues appear to be driving the field: the economy and crime. These issues are nothing new. It seems that each election cycle over the past few years has had one or both of these issues on the table.

This election cycle, however, has other issues before the public that makes this no ordinary time.

Recall an election years ago. The main issues were the economy and crime. Out of the political give-and-take there emerged a charismatic figure who promised to restore the country to greatness.

No, it wasn't Bill Clinton or Donald Trump.

It was Adolf Hitler.

In October of 1929, a worldwide depression began, forcing businesses to decrease production and lay off workers. Germany felt the effects of the depression almost immediately. By 1932, 6 million Germans were unemployed in a nation of about 60 million people.

During 1930–1933, the mood in Germany was grim. The unemployed were joined by millions of others who linked the Depression to Germany's national humiliation after defeat in World War 1. Many Germans perceived the parliamentary government coalition as weak and unable to alleviate the economic crisis. Widespread economic misery, fear, and perception of worse times to come, as well as anger and impatience with the apparent failure of the government to manage the crisis, offered fertile ground for the rise of Adolf Hitler and his Nazi Party.

First, they said, Germany did not lose World War I, but was betrayed into losing the war. Usually, the corollary to that was that the leftists and Jews betrayed them.

Second, the parliamentary democracy set up after the war to run Germany, the Weimar Republic, was hopelessly unwieldy and inefficient.

Third was a call to law and order. German culture abhors chaos and if nothing else post-war Germany was chaotic. Therefore, the several parties appealed to the German peoples' sense of law and order; the attitude being it's better to have an autocratic regime than allowing the chaos to continue.

Any of this sound familiar? Note that the frequency of Anti-Semitism has increased dramatically over the past few years.

People generally vote their pocketbooks and wallets. History bears this out. Voters want the party in power that will solve their economic woes and make it safe to walk the streets. If one party had all the answers, though, we wouldn't be switching from Democrat to Republican and back again as frequently as we do.

When the economy is sour, the party in power takes the hit. Just look at Bill Clinton's victory over incumbent President George Bush in 1992. Of course, there were other factors, most notably Ross Perot's strong third party showing. But the Democrats' slogan for that campaign was "It's the economy, stupid." And it was the economy that sent Clinton to the White House.

The reality is neither party has all the answers. Sometimes we wonder if they truly understand the questions. But we are a two-party country and we get what we vote for.

So, it's important to know precisely what we're about to vote for.

Let's take the two major issues of the economy and street crime.

Assuming the Republicans sweep Congress, what will they do to improve the economy? They will continue to give huge tax breaks to the wealthy. They will either increase taxes on the middle class to pay for social service programs, or reduce those programs. Among the programs targeted by Republicans for privatization or sunset and possible re-enactment are the bedrock safety nets of Social Security and Medicare. In the name of fiscal responsibility, they will continue to insist on permanent tax breaks for the wealthy, with any tax increase foisted on the middle class.

Republicans who are on Social Security and Medicare take note. Ask yourselves if this is what you really want. Do you want your Social Security payments and Medicare benefits impacted by your party leaders? That is one of the promises the party leadership made during the current campaign.

How will the Republicans handle street crime? By hiring more police, and keeping criminals locked up longer. And how will the hiring of more police officers, and building more prisons to house and care for more inmates, be paid for? By taxes on the middle class or by cutting social services that are designed in part to keep people from committing crimes in the first place.

We can readily agree that there are too many mass shootings and too many lives needlessly lost. But it's the Republican Party that continues to object to any legislation to curb mass shootings, such as banning assault weapons, under the rubric of protecting the rights of law-abiding citizens. There is no right for anyone to own or possess an assault weapon. There is no doubt that easy access to weapons of mass murder is a factor in these mass shootings. Just don't expect the Republican Party to do anything about this; they're too busy supporting open carry laws allowing people to carry weapons in public places.

We can expect Republicans to continue telling teachers what they can and can't teach; students what they can and can't study; businesses what they can and can't say about government practices; universities and colleges what they can and can't teach; college students what they can and can't say or learn. Despite claiming to empower parents to make decisions for their children, the Republican Party will continue to take it upon itself to decide what books to ban and what can be taught.

We can expect Republicans to ignore investigations of Donald Trump and his congressional allies, as well as those embarrassing claims against Herschel Walker, as other candidates of questionable character and qualifications. They will do this in the name of family values.

We can expect Republicans to continue waxing on limited government even as some, including former VP Mike Pence, have made it their mission to place the primacy of the Christian religion in government, to the point of forcing that religion on others who believe differently. This is not limited government; it's the promise of theocracy where one religion superintends government and those who have different beliefs.

We can expect Republicans, in the name of the rule of law, to stop investigations into repeated election lies, election denials, refusing to accept election results, stealing government records, subpoena snubs, pardon pleas, threatening violence if criminal charges are filed, etc.

We can expect Republicans, in the name of peace through strength, to support Russian despot Vladimir Putin in his war against Ukraine, and his verbal assault against our nation's most important allies in NATO.

We can expect Republicans to continue their push for free markets, ignoring the history of businesses operating without restriction or limitation. History is clear about what happens when businesses run amok without government oversight. We need only look to the Great Depression of 1929 and the Great Meltdown of 2008.

We can expect Republicans to continue their claim of supporting human dignity by restricting the words and actions of women, educators, students, businesses, etc., who refuse to kowtow to the party line. Human dignity is not fostered by ending or turning over Social Security and Medicare to the whims (and greed) of the big corporations.

As I said previously, this is also no ordinary time. This election cycle, and the next one, are about a seismic shift in the foundation of our government. The Republicans have made it clear that Christian nationalism should be the rule and guide to our government. They believe that one religion can force its doctrine and dogma on others, despite the nation's history of religious tolerance. That alone should be a disqualifier, but sadly, it's not. Rather, it's a rallying cry for the Christian nationalists that control the party's message and platform.

Given a free hand, Republicans on the far right will move the country toward an authoritarian form not unlike what we witnessed in Germany in the early 1930s. History doesn't lie; its lessons are there for us to learn, or ignore at our peril.

So, in search of solutions, be careful what you vote for. The cure may be far worse than the illness.

"LOVE WILL KEEP US TOGETHER": SONGS SEND A POWERFUL MESSAGE

"Antisemitism is … on the rise on the American right in what looks like outreach to those embracing European-style fascism. Former president Trump recently warned American Jews to "get their act together" and show more support for Israel "before it is too late," while the recent outbursts from artist Ye (also known as Kanye West) have led Adidas to cancel its contract with him and upended his other projects. In Pennsylvania the Republican candidate for governor, Doug Mastriano, a right-wing Christian who opposes the separation of church and state, has made attacking the Jewish faith of his Democratic opponent, Attorney General Josh Shapiro, a big part of his campaign." –Author and Historian Heather Cox Richardson, October 27, 2022.

"All you need is love
All you need is love
All you need is love, love
Love is all you need."

Discrimination is a prominent and critically important matter in American life, with significant and harmful effects on health and well-being. The largest poll of its kind conducted to date, "Discrimination in America" focuses on personal experiences with discrimination across more than a dozen areas of daily life. Key findings are:

Nearly half (45%) of African Americans experienced racial discrimination when trying to rent an apartment or buy a home.
18% of Asian Americans say they have experienced discrimination when interacting with police. Indian-Americans are much more likely than Chinese-Americans to report unfair police stops or treatment.
Nearly 1 in 5 Latinos have avoided medical care due to concern of being discriminated against or treated poorly.
34% of LGBTQ Americans say they that they or a friend have been verbally harassed while using the restroom.
41% of women report being discriminated against in equal pay and promotion opportunities.

"What the world needs now,
Is love, sweet love,
It's the only thing that there's just too little of.
What the world needs now,
Is love, sweet love,
No, not just for some but for everyone."

"Blacks and Jews have a unique, powerful and, sadly, generational relationship with persecution. In many ways, particularly during the civil rights movement, we have long been allies, brothers and sisters. There's a historic, loving and empathetic connection between our communities. It's a connection that has been tested at times – and not always flawless – but has remained close, especially now, during the racism of the Trump era. It cannot be overstated how destructive (Kanye West) Ye is to this unity and to race relations overall. He is one of the most popular celebrities alive, with tens of millions of social media followers. People, for various reasons, for reasons I will never comprehend, listen to what he says.

Most important, other antisemites are utilizing Ye not solely as a dividing force, but the Black face of one. ... Ye's journey into hate comes at a frightening time in America. If you haven't been paying attention, this is a scary moment for Jews. The persecution they face isn't theoretical. It is real and disturbing, and so much of it is being pushed by right-wing extremists in the media, entertainment and politics.

The Anti-Defamation League reported in April that antisemitic incidents reached an all-time high in the United States in 2021, with a total of 2,717 incidents of assault, harassment and vandalism. This represents the highest number of incidents on record since the ADL began tracking such data in 1979, the organization said.

It's not just the numbers or the violence. It's two other factors: the openness of the bigotry, and how Ye is a rallying cry for racists. ...

When (public officials) or a star Black rapper is openly racist against Jews, it opens up massive permission structures for others. They replicate like viruses. I haven't felt or seen anything in my lifetime like the current levels of open white nationalism we're witnessing now. While it's directed against many people, it has become laser-focused on the Jewish community.

Antisemitism is something everyone needs to condemn in the strongest terms … . There should be no acceptance, of any kind, of antisemitism. Banish the racists to the litter box of history. Never forgive them. Never forget them." --USA Today Columnist Mike Freeman. October 28, 2022.

"And how many years can some people exist
Before they're allowed to be free?

Yes, and how many times can a man turn his head
And pretend that he just doesn't see?
The answer, my friend, is blowin' in the wind
The answer is blowin' in the wind

Yes, and how many times must a man look up
Before he can see the sky?
And how many ears must one man have
Before he can hear people cry?

Yes, and how many deaths will it take 'til he knows
That too many people have died?
The answer, my friend, is blowin' in the wind
The answer is blowin' in the wind."

"Hatred is a Cancer Growing on America. … While history's pages are strewn with many examples of hate and its painful impact, two of our nation's most recent examples come to mind: the slaughter of innocent men and women at a prayer meeting in a predominantly Black church in Charleston, SC in 2015 and (the 2018) slaying of 11 Jewish men and women at a Synagogue in Pittsburgh, PA.

In both of these cases, the attackers chose their targets for death for no apparent reason other than who they were and the fact both men considered their targets to be different or less worthy of life than themselves or other people who they perceived to be more like them in skin color or religious affiliation. Neither shooter had any apparent personal knowledge of anyone they killed. No perceived slight. No grudge. Nothing, except for the perception the people targeted were not worthy of living an American life of liberty and happiness. ... This kind of hatred is bred into us by ...someone ...who has a whole different personality we've seen come out in recent years."--Robert M. Williams, Jr., former editor and publisher, Blackshear Times (2018).

"Think of your fellow man, lend him a helping hand
Put a little love in your heart
You see, it's getting late, oh, please don't hesitate
Put a little love in your heart
And the world will be a better place
And the world will be a better place for you and me
You just wait and see

Another day goes by, and still the children cry
Put a little love in your heart

If you want the world to know, we won't let hatred grow
Put a little love in your heart
And the world will be a better place
And the world will be a better place for you and me
You just wait and see, wait and see

Take a good look around and if you're lookin' down
Put a little love in your heart, yeah
I hope when you decide kindness will be your guide
Put a little love in your heart
And the world will be a better place
And the world will be a better place for you and me
You just wait and see."

Here we are in the third decade of the 21st century and hardly a day goes by that we don't read or hear about an attack or demonstration based on nothing more than hatred, bigotry and prejudice.

"Imagine all the people
Livin' life in peace."

"Oh, When will (we) ever learn?
Oh, When will (we) ever learn."

REPUBLICANS CONTINUE TO RELY ON A
WARPED, REVISIONIST VIEW OF THE REAL
HISTORY OF THE TWO MAJOR POLITICAL
PARTIES, AND THE PERCEPTION OF
INCREASED CRIME.

Author and Historian Heather Cox Richardson sets the
record straight on the history of the two major political
parties. Today, many Republicans glaringly ignore the
parties' shift in the 1960s over race and civil rights. As
Richardson says: "Republican candidate for Michigan
governor Tudor Dixon said that the Democrats have planned
for decades to topple the United States because they have
not gotten over losing the Civil War.

According to Dixon, Democrats don't want anyone to
know that white Republicans freed the slaves, and are
deliberately strangling 'true history.'" Dixon was harping
on an oft-repeated theme "that Democrats were the party of
enslavement, Republicans pushed emancipation, and thus
the whole idea that Republican policies today are bad for
Black Americans is disinformation." Many Republicans are
also told that it was the GOP that freed the slaves.

In reality, what Dixon said is a 180-degree shift from, or
complete reversal of, the true historical record. The fact
is, as Richardson notes, "the parties have switched sides
since the 1850s. The shift happened in the 1960s, and it
happened over the issue of race" Richardson encapsulates
that immutable history in her column. Those who rely

on this warped and erroneous history of the two major parties as spun by Dixon and her ilk do a disservice to all Americans who deserve to be told the unvarnished and fully documented truth. But so long as the party faithful believe this great lie, Republicans like Dixon will continue to tell it. They evidently believe, as Adolph Hitler's propaganda minister Joseph Goebbels believed: A lie repeated often enough is the truth.

Republicans have made great headway on the issue of crime. Recent statistics, however, reveal that it's not the reality of the crime rates that is scoring major points for Republican candidates leading up to the November 8 elections. Rather, it's the perception and fear of crime that is the party's driving force. Democrats have been forced to defend the charge that they want to defund the police. They don't, but that doesn't matter. People are scared; fear is a great motivator, and instilling fear about crime is advantage Republicans.

FLORIDA IS A LEADER IN BANNED BOOKS. IS THIS LEADERSHIP?

I abhor banning books. Books are sources of knowledge and information. Historians note that banning them is the first sign of a slide toward totalitarianism.

Banning books restricts information and discourages freedom of thought. Those who censor undermine one of the primary functions of education: teaching students how to think for themselves. Such actions, free speech proponents say, endanger tolerance, free expression, and democracy. For teachers, book banning means shaky, ever-changing curriculum, fear for personal choices, and the tragedy of self-censorship. For students, book banning means a denial of First Amendment rights, a narrow world view, and psychological deficits. For the classroom, book banning means discourse is hindered.

The presumption must always favor publication; book banning should be a rarity and occur only upon proof by clear and convincing evidence that a book presents a clear and present danger to the community at large. Standards must be uniform and not subject to personal likes or dislikes of the censors. For a book to be banned, there must be a clear avenue for appealing a local decision, and the procedures must be clearly set out and available to all, much like rules governing the practice of law and the judiciary.

This is not to say that book banning should never occur. There are certainly limited areas where banning books is appropriate. Books that describe how to make a bomb or disclose highly classified information that creates a clear and present danger to safety and life come immediately to mind.

The most glaring problem with book bans is the real tendency to overreach. Once the censors take their pen to their list and start striking though book titles, it becomes easier and easier to add more to that expanding list.

PEN America, a nonprofit group that advocates for free expression in literature, notes that over the 2021–22 school year, what started as modest school-level activity to challenge and remove books in schools grew into a full-fledged social and political movement. This group also reports that Florida is among the states with the most book bans.

PEN America notes that Florida has book bans in 21 of the state's school districts involving 566 titles. The majority of banned books contain themes or characters involving the LGBTQ community and people of color.

The report also says most of the bans have been pushed by about 50 groups, including Moms for Liberty -- a parental rights group founded in Florida -- and the Florida Citizens Alliance. In St. Lucie County Schools, a complainant submitted official reconsideration challenges for 44 titles from the FLC's "Porn in Schools" report.

After reading the reasons for banning certain books in a certain article, I didn't know whether to laugh at the stupidity or cry at the ignorance.

Keri Blakinger is a journalist for the Marshall Project, an online journalism organization focusing on issues related to criminal justice in the United States. She wrote a book about her experiences.

"It's kind of hilarious that the prison system — now that I am rehabilitated and doing good things in the world — says that my writing is dangerously inflammatory," she told NPR. "I also think it's absurd that one of the reasons for the ban was that the book presents 'a threat to the security, order or rehabilitative objectives of the correctional system.' The book is literally a story about rehabilitation.

"Texas has banned The Color Purple. Michigan bans Dungeons and Dragons books," she said, referring to the famous tabletop fantasy roleplaying game.

Michigan has also banned dictionaries in Spanish and Swahili under claims that the books' contents are a threat to the state's penitentiaries. Prison officials said they feared inmates would learn an "obscure language" and organize against staff.

Oddly enough, Blakinger has found books championing extremism and white supremacy like The Turner Diaries and Adolf Hitler's Mein Kampf are rarely prohibited in prison.

You can see how easy it is to add books to the banned list once the banning starts.

According to Florida Today, there are 263 books banned in Florida prisons.

I read the two lists of banned books—the state school districts and Florida prisons—and couldn't find Mein Kampf or The Turner Diaries on either one.

For your information, the 13 criteria used to decide which books to ban from Florida's prisons are as follows:

3A Describes construction or use of weapons, ammunition, bombs, chemical agents or incendiary devices

3B   Describes methods of escape; contains blueprints, drawings or descriptions of corrections facilities; includes road maps that can facilitate escape.

3C   Describes procedures for the brewing of alcoholic beverages or the manufacture of drugs.

3D   Written in code or is otherwise not reasonably subject to interpretation by staff.

3E   Depicts activities which may lead to physical violence or group disruption.

3F   Encourages or instructs in commission of criminal activity.

3G   Dangerously inflammatory -- encourages riot, insurrection, disruption of the institution, violation of rules.

3H   Threatens physical harm, blackmail or extortion.

3I   Depicts sexual conduct.

3J   Depicts nudity in a way to create the appearance that sexual conduct is imminent.

3K   Contains criminal history or other personal information about another inmate.

3L   Contains an ad promoting three-way calling services, pen pal services, purchase of products or services with postage stamps, or conducting a business while incarcerated.

3M   It otherwise presents a threat to the security, order or rehabilitative objectives of the correctional system or the safety of any person.

TOM BRADY WASHED UP? HARDLY.

For the past few weeks, I've listened to pro football pundits talking about Tom Brady's final collapse into mediocrity, a shell of his former self as the greatest of all time. After the latest round of Brady bashing, I decided to check the numbers.

Brady has played in 326 regular season games, passing for 86,787 yards. That averages out to 266 yards per game for more than 20 years. This year, in 8 games, he's passed for 2,267 yards, for an average of 283 yards a game--certainly not an over-the-hill stat. He has thrown 9 TD passes and only 1 interception.

Sure, the Bucs have a losing record, and it's easy to blame a QB who's defying Father Time by playing at a high level at age 45, something that hasn't been done before. But Brady can't run or catch the ball; and when backs don't do well, and receivers drop balls, pundits--especially the I-told-you-so kind--blame the QB.

As fans, let's focus on what we won't see again in our lifetime--a singularly gifted athlete who, instead of looking like a grizzly old football player (Brett Favre, Y. A. Tittle and George Blanda come to mind), looks like he just stepped out of a GQ modeling session.

FRUSTRATION MOUNTS.

We are in a place I never thought we'd be in at this stage of the 21st century. And there's a feeling of helplessness. Reality, facts, etc., don't seem to matter. It's more about rage, vengeance and violence. Seemingly daily shootings make us think twice about going out; climate change's effects on our lives and property, and on and on. We seem to be too busy bashing and not spending nearly enough time tackling problems that may very soon become insurmountable. There seems to be an attitude of living for today, not worrying about tomorrow. The fact is tomorrow has arrived.

For the better part of two years, I've been writing essays of varying lengths dealing with what I see as the direction our nation is taking. After more than 400 of them, I am reaching the point of sheer exhaustion.

It's like loudly knocking on the door, only to find there's no one at home....or the homeowner isn't hearing it. I've had a few tell me I don't know what I'm talking about, yet I've not had a single person refute the facts I offer, or provide me with facts refuting mine. What I get in response to my challenge to them is more anger and more accusations. This isn't healthy for a Democracy, but that doesn't matter.

They're right and the rest of us are wrong, and you can't argue with that mindset.

The common ground is fact and logic; if fact is trashed, then logic becomes whatever is in the mind of the beholder. When belief becomes fact, there can be no common ground except among similar believers. This is how conspiracy theories develop and metastasize. Someone believes that something is true because he/she possesses information not available to others, so the belief goes. Like Pizzagate, a wild eyed debunked belief that the Democrats were running a Satanic cult baby-killing operation out of a pizza parlor basement in Washington, D.C. Through social media, this nonsense spread like a cancer. In fact, conspiracy theories spread like wildfire because one person's belief becomes readily accepted by others who believe that what they get on social media is reality rather than misinformation and downright craziness and nonsense. Try finding common ground with that mentality.

I've been accused of lacking common sense and rational thinking by those who are election deniers, believe the January 6 attack on the capital was either a result of Antifa or nothing more than a few folks engaging in legitimate political discourse, see nothing wrong with stealing government records, etc. I wonder how many agree with anti-Semitic comments made recently. The point again is that you can't engage in meaningful dialogue with those who have these beliefs.

There are folks who ask where are the sane, deep-thinking Republicans with whom we can converse in an effort to find common ground. Sadly, they have been shunted to the side, fearful of speaking out and further inflame the far right. It's possible for people to make new decisions when presented with new information; they must, however, be willing to accept new information that goes against their mindset. It's hard for people to admit error and change their minds.

The problem is compounded, however, when people are fed a steady stream of disinformation, including lies and conspiracy theories. Remember that a conspiracy theory, like a lie, will travel around the world while the truth is getting its boots on.

Why people choose to believe a lie or conspiracy theory is a matter for psychologists to explain. They may be more interesting or intriguing than the truth. It may a matter of how the brain functions when told a lie or a wild baseless theory.

SEN. LINDSEY GRAHAM MUST TESTIFY UNDER OATH BEFORE GEORGIA OFFICIALS INVESTIGATING ATTEMPTS TO INFLUENCE THE 2020 PRESIDENTIAL ELECTION RESULTS.

Sen. Lindsey Graham has just had his options limited by the Supreme Court. He is now under subpoena to testify under oath in connection with efforts directed to the Georgia results of the 2020 presidential election. You might recall Donald Trump's call to the Georgia secretary of state imploring him to find enough votes to declare Trump the winner of the state's electoral college votes.

Well, Sen. Graham might have also played a role in that effort, and that's what the Fulton County district attorney and the grand jury are investigating.

Graham, in attempting to avoid having to testify, claimed that as a sitting senator, the Constitution's "speech and debate" clause protects him, as a member of Congress, from having to worry that anything he says in the course of legislative activities will implicate him in a lawsuit.

What is fair game for inquiry, however, are attempts to change the results of an election, or interfere in the outcome of a fair and honest election. Specifically, Georgia officials want to see if Graham attempted to unduly influence election officials in the performance of their duties. Perhaps there's a connection between what Trump tried to accomplish in a phone call to the Georgia secretary of state that was recorded, and what Graham hoped to accomplish by his contacts with those same officials. That was the call in which Trump said "I just want to find 11,780 votes, which is one more than we have [to get]" to surpass Biden's total.

Since Graham must now testify under oath, it seems he has three legitimate options: plead the Fifth Amendment right against self-incrimination; claim every question asked is protected by the "speech and debate" clause; or tell the truth.

Graham has to know--or at least his lawyers must know--that the Georgia officials have a wealth of evidence and testimony under oath already in hand. Further, they have already specifically tailored their questions to what Graham said and did completely separate and apart from what is covered by the "speech and debate" clause.

If he pleads the Fifth Amendment, Graham runs the risk of offering nothing to counter the evidence Georgia officials already have. If he objects to each question on "speech and debate" grounds, he faces the same prospects of offering nothing to counter the state's evidence. These two efforts would possibly drag out the proceeding; however, since the state officials have evidence and testimony in hand, they could move forward without Graham's testimony.

He could, of course, lie under oath, but that's perjury, a felony. If he offers answers that he represents as the truth, his story will undoubtedly run counter to statements already provided to those state officials.

Interesting times ahead indeed for Sen. Graham.

THE DEEP STATE AND "AMERICAN RESISTANCE."

Of the more than a dozen books written about Donald Trump that portray him in a negative light—authoritarian, anti-Democratic, putting himself above the country, lawbreaker, etc.—perhaps none is more intriguing than the recently released "American Resistance" by David Rothkopf. Rothkopf is a foreign policy, national security and political affairs analyst and commentator; this is his seventh book.

With the publication of each of these damning books, Trump typically rants about "fake news," "witch hunt," "a hatchet job" that is "full of lies," etc. One would think that with all these books portraying Trump in a bad light, he would have been quite successful in suing these authors for defamation. Yet, there is no report by him or his friends in the media of any lawsuit that has been successful.

Surely, if he's right, it wouldn't be difficult for his lawyers to prove these authors knew what they were writing about was false, or published their books with reckless disregard for the truth. If Trump has the facts to support his version of the truth, winning a defamation case against these authors would be child's play for the self-proclaimed "stable genius." And the same would be true for media reporters, editors and publishers who have disclosed unsavory things about Trump—and continue to do so even as he is no longer a public official.

That there have been no successful lawsuits says a lot about what has been reported, and the absence of a factual foundation for the typical Trump claims.

For several years, Trump has lashed out at the "deep state" as the source of his predicaments. He's not the first president to criticize the government over which he presided. Whether it was denigrated as "the bureaucracy" or as Ronald Reagan famously said *"Government is not the solution to our problem, government is the problem.,"* that unseen but carefully crafted image of a government run amok has deeply implanted into the public conscience—and through FOX News, NewsMax, Breitbart, Infowars, etc.—this effort continues.

The deep state was first equating with "the steady creep of government bureaucracy that drains the vitality and wealth of the people." However, Trump's presidency, aided by right wing media, conjured up the "deep state" as something far more sinister. More than just signifying an impersonal, inept bureaucracy, it conjures up a secretive illuminati of bureaucrats determined to sabotage the Trump agenda and Trumpism generally. Their scapegoats abound; we see evidence of that quite clearly today.

Well, it turns out that, according to Rothkopf, there was a deep state during Trump's four years. But not the sinister, evildoers as portrayed by the extreme right; rather, the Trump-era deep state comes from "most of the people who work in the US government (who) are actually fundamentally good, well intentioned, and trying to make a positive difference for America."

The author discusses a few Washington officials who resisted the risk to the nation by an unprecedented presidency. Through their efforts, Rothkopf writes, they prevented the kind of chaos that could have overwhelmed our government and the nation.

As the author notes, each federal employee takes an oath to "support and defend the Constitution of the United States against all enemies foreign and domestic," but none had imagined that enemy might be the president himself. "With the presidency of Donald Trump, a fault line between the president and vital forces within his government was established. Those who honored their oath of office, their obligation to the Constitution, were wary of the president and they in turn were not trusted and occasionally fired and replaced with loyalists."

This is Rothkopf's narrative, and is called the first book to chronicle the unprecedented role so many in the government were forced to play, and the consequences of their actions during the Trump administration. From Lt. Col. Alexander Vindman and his brother Yevgeny, to Ambassador Marie Yovanovitch, to Bill Taylor, Fiona Hill, and the official who first called himself "Anonymous"—Miles Taylor, among others. Some of these names might be familiar to those who followed the televised hearings this past summer of the House committee investigating the January 6 attack on the capital.

"Rothkopf examines the resistance movement that slowly built in Washington (from 2017). Drawing from firsthand testimonies, deep background and research, American Resistance shows how when the President threatened to run amok, a few key figures rose in defiance. It reveals the conflict within the Department of Justice over actively seeking instances of election fraud and abuse to help the president illegally retain power, and multiple battles within the White House over the influence of Jared and Ivanka, and in particular the extraordinary efforts to get them security clearances even after they were denied to them."

Rothkopf chronicles how each person came to realize that they were working for an administration that threatened to wreak havoc; one Defense Secretary was told by his mother to resign before it was too late.

This narrative recalls a quote attributable to Edmund Burke: "The only thing *necessary for the triumph of evil* is for good men to do nothing."

Rothkopf shows how a few good men and women who took their oaths to heart stood up to the authoritarian in their midst. These people are the true patriots.

INTERESTING HISTORICAL INFORMATION ABOUT OUR PRESIDENTS OVER THE PAST 100 YEARS.

This is interesting. In the last 100 years, we have had 16 presidents---8 Republicans (Hoover, Eisenhower, Nixon, Ford, Reagan, Bush, Bush, Trump), 8 Democrats (Roosevelt, Truman, Kennedy, Johnson, Carter, Clinton, Obama, Biden). Republicans had moderates (Nixon, Ford) and conservatives

(Hoover, Reagan, Bush, Bush and Trump); Democrats had liberals (Roosevelt, Truman, Kennedy, Johnson, Obama) and moderates (Carter, Clinton)--although they differ on the political sliding scale from the center going left or right.

Presidents like to reflect on the will of the people. With this equal shift between parties and political philosophy, what does this tell us about the will of the people over the past century? It looks as if voters don't want much of a continuation of one party in the White House for too long, unless conditions and circumstances warrant it.

Herbert Hoover botched the economy, leading to 20 years of liberalism via Roosevelt and Truman. But that was enough, and Dwight Eisenhower represented a respite and a grandfatherly touch. But after eight years, people wanted someone young and refreshing, and found it in John Kennedy. Lyndon Johnson took over for the assassinated JFK and ushered in an FDR-type of leadership, pushing for civil rights and voting rights legislation. But the Vietnam War was his undoing, and Richard Nixon was elected. He, however, had his own problems, most notably Watergate, so his hand-picked VP Gerald Ford took over. Voters, however, had enough of Nixon-Ford and the latter's pardon of the former, so the voters chose Jimmy Carter.

But Carter proved a disappointment, so the voters chose the charismatic former actor and California governor Ronald Reagan. Reagan ushered in a modern-day conservatism that carried over to George Bush, even in the shadow of

Iran-Contra. However, Bush's handling of the economy opened the door for another young and charismatic candidate, former Arkansas governor Bill Clinton. But he had his own personal issues with young ladies, and after eight years, voters had enough and switched again, this time to George Bush, son of the former president.

After eight years and Mideast issues along with an economic meltdown, however, voters tried something entirely different, electing the first African-American president, Barack Obama. But his eight years of liberalism led to another drastic departure, the election of the first president without a single day of public service, Donald Trump. For many reasons, four years of Trump was enough, so the voters turned to an old warhorse, Joe Biden. Whether voters sour on him as they have on some of his predecessors remains to be seen.

Perhaps, in the last analysis, Americans really don't know what they want, but whatever it is, it's not what they have at any given time.

AN ELECTION LIKE NO OTHER

"60 Percent Of Americans Will Have An Election Denier On The Ballot This Fall."

This is the headline of an article published by FiveThirtyEight, an American website that focuses on opinion poll analysis, politics, economics, and sports blogging in the United States.

According to FiveThirtyEight, "out of 552 total Republican nominees running for office, we found 199 who fully deny the legitimacy of the 2020 election. These candidates either clearly stated that the election was stolen from Trump or took legal action to overturn the results, such as voting not to certify election results or joining lawsuits that sought to overturn the election.

Moreover, an additional 61 candidates raised questions (about) the results of the 2020 election. These candidates haven't gone so far as to say explicitly that the election was stolen or take legal action to overturn it. However, they haven't said the election was legitimate either. In fact, they have raised doubts about potential fraud."

Another 122 Republican candidates refused to respond to the survey.

"A total of 77 have fully accepted the results of the 2020 election while another 93 have accepted with reservations, meaning they think President Biden won, but still raised concerns about the integrity of the election."

To further show the pervasive control Donald Trump has over these Republican candidates, a growing number of candidates refuse to acknowledge the legitimacy of the upcoming election results unless they win.

Arizona is the ground zero of the 2022 threat of election subversion. All four of its Republican candidates in statewide races –governor, senate, attorney general and secretary of state – are out-and-out election deniers and refuseniks.

If this were not enough, there are many Republican deniers and refuseniks who are candidates for offices that supervise elections, and polls indicate many will be successful. Imagine having the states' election system in the hands of those who refuse to recognize the legitimate outcome of one election and further refuse to acknowledge future results unless their party's candidates win! Those who are successful will be in charge of a system they won't honor or respect unless their candidates win!

Americans should be outraged over such a prospect. Sadly, one political party believes this is perfectly acceptable behavior.

These candidates of a major American political party persist in their denials and refusals without a shred of supporting evidence, solely because their cult leader refuses to publicly acknowledge what he has recognized privately-- the fact that he lost in 2020, and is now willing to take a knife to the most fundamental right in a Democratic society.

Former united nations Secretary-General Kofi Annan summed it up well recently: "Elections are at the heart of democracy. When conducted with integrity, they allow citizens to have a voice in how and by whom they are governed. This is because while human beings need security and livelihoods, they also need freedom, dignity and justice."

If these candidates are unwilling to accept the 2020 election, and further refuse to acknowledge the results of the November elections unless they win—and base their refusal on belief without a shred of supporting evidence—it is a legitimate question whether these candidates really support our form of government.

It wasn't very long ago that we had the closest presidential election in our nation's history.

In 2000, George Bush beat Al Gore by 527 votes in Florida. That vote gave Bush the state's electoral college vote that put him over the 270 needed for victory.

Gore, the sitting vice president, didn't claim the election was rigged. He didn't tell his supporters to march to the capital to stop the certification of the electoral college results, by violence if necessary, calling the rioters patriots. In fact, he presided over that certification process, just as Mike Pence did in 2020. Gore didn't refuse to show up at Bush's inauguration. He didn't persist in lying about the result years afterwards. And he didn't bend his party's officeholders and candidates to his will in denying the 2000 election results and compel them to refuse to acknowledge future election results unless they win.

The Democrats had the chance to do everything Trump has done to poison our electoral system. Rather than resort to lies, rage, anger and violence, they chose to honor our Constitution and our democratic form of government that compels recognition of the will of the people.

For Al Gore, it was about our time-honored system of elections and governance. For Donald Trump, it's all about him. The comparison between how the major political parties handled close elections couldn't be more profound.

Because there are so many deniers and refuseniks running under the Republican banner—and polls indicate a number of them will be elected—it can be said that this will be an election like no other.

What does this portend for future elections?

REPUBLICANS' CAMPAIGN IS BASED ON THREE MYTHS.

As the November midterm elections draw close, it's important to consider the three major issues that seem to be driving the polls that favor the Republican Party.

The three core issues are the economy, crime and socialism.

As you will see, each of these issues is based on a myth.

Myth No. 1: <u>"The economy is tanking, and it's all Joe Biden's and the Democrats' fault."</u>

Certainly the economy is in the driver's seat when it comes to campaign issues. When the economy is bad—rising prices, stagnant wages, etc.—the party in power takes the blame. And the cost of gas at the pump lies at the heart of the Republicans' campaign theme.

But here is the question they deftly avoid: how much control does the president actually have over the price of oil? Virtually none. Gasoline prices are determined largely by the laws of supply and demand. These prices cover the cost of acquiring and refining crude oil as well as distributing and marketing the gasoline, in addition to state and federal taxes. Gas prices also respond to geopolitical events that impact the oil market. What must also be factored in for this election is the effect the global COVID pandemic has had on oil prices. The bottom line is that the president has virtually no control over gas prices.

The president can request action by Congress to raise or lower the taxes and tariffs on oil and gasoline, and has some congressionally granted regulatory power as the head of the executive branch of government, but that power is very limited without congressional approval. Expecting the current Congress to act in support of a president of the opposition party is expecting far too much.

What about price controls? Setting price controls for food, gas, cars and services have been tried before, typically during times of crisis, but for most mainstream economists, the answer to this question is a resounding "no." Limiting how much companies can charge will distort markets, they argue, causing shortages and exacerbating supply chain problems while only temporarily reducing inflation.

And if a Democratic president undertook any unilateral effort to control prices, there would be a hue and cry from Republicans over government control over private enterprise—something they would never allow to happen.

Myth No. 2: "Democrats are soft on crime."

What is initially important here is the type of crime Republicans are talking about. They are most assuredly not talking about white collar crimes: corporate greed that flowed from Republican-led unregulated markets; the economic collapses of the Great Depression of the 1930s or the Great Meltdown and "too big to fail" mentality of 2008 when millions of Americans lost their life savings and their jobs; the Bernie Madoffs and Ponzi schemes; the Enrons and other vivid examples of the worst of the combination of unaccountable markets meeting pure avarice.

No, the Republicans will never talk about corporate white collar crime because it cuts against their free market platform. Nor will they talk about crime involving public officials in the Republican Party--starting at the top and in the White House from 2017-2021, and elsewhere among party loyalists.

With perfectly good reasons, they would prefer that their constituents focus on street crime.

Republicans have portrayed Democrats as soft on crime, attacking them over policies such as bail reform, which seeks to prevent defendants charged with nonviolent crimes from being held indefinitely. But experts say local public policy changes have little effect on overall crime trends.

According to Thomas Abt, chairman of the Council on Criminal Justice, "The problem with all of these conservative critiques is that crime went up everywhere. It went up in red states, it went up in blue states, it went up in cities controlled by Republican mayors and cities controlled by Democratic mayors. It went up in cities, also in the suburbs, also in rural areas."

Public perception of crime is often at odds with the raw statistics. Opinion polls typically find Americans believe crime is a bigger problem nationally than in their own neighborhoods, even though crime broadly tends to rise and fall across geographical lines.

Despite politicized claims that this rise was the result of criminal justice reform in liberal-leaning jurisdictions, murders rose roughly equally in cities run by Republicans and cities run by Democrats. So-called "red" states actually saw some of the highest murder rates of all. This data makes it difficult to pin recent trends on local policy shifts and reveals the basic inaccuracy of attempts to politicize a problem as complex as crime. Instead, the evidence points to broad national causes driving rising crime.

Third Way is a centrist political position that attempts to reconcile right-wing and left-wing politics by advocating a varying synthesis of center-right economic policies with center-left social policies.

Third Way notes that Trump-voting states accounted for 8 out of the 10 highest murder rates in 2020. "If you're tuned in to the media, you'd think murder is rocketing skyward in New York, California, Illinois. But those states don't even crack the top ten. In fact, the top per capita murder rate states in 2020 were mostly those far from massive urban centers and Democratic mayors and governors. Eight of the top ten worst murder rate states voted for Trump in 2020. None of those eight has supported a Democrat for president since 1996."

According to Third Way, "Mississippi had the highest homicide rate at 20.50 murders per 100,000 residents, followed by Louisiana at 15.79, Kentucky at 14.32, Alabama at 14.2, and Missouri at 14. The national average was 6.5 per 100,000 residents, but the top five states had rates more than twice that high. The rest of the top ten were South Carolina, New Mexico, Georgia, Arkansas, and Tennessee. ... Notably, New Mexico and Georgia were the only Biden-voting states in the top ten, and they ranked seventh and eighth, respectively."

3. Myth No. 3: "Stop the Democrats' advance to Socialism."

America has never been—and never will be--a socialist country. To be sure, America had socialist-type programs born of necessity in the 1930s when 12 years of free markets championed by the Republican Party precipitated the Stock Market Crash of 1929 and the Great Depression of following decade. To stem the staggering, unprecedented losses, the Franklin Roosevelt Administration sought legislative enactment of an economic safety net, the reining in of lending institutions and the securities markets, and passage of programs designed to put people back to work, among other New Deal programs designed to save the nation's economy, and the nation itself.

Even as more and more Americans were suffering; as the lines for food grew longer; as more and more lost everything, President Herbert Hoover maintained the view that the markets would regulate themselves toward correctness. He was wrong; and his approach led to much needless suffering. We can only wonder what might have been had the Republicans' fixation on free, unregulated markets carried the day during the 1930s. History is clear: 1929 and 2008 demonstrate that unregulated markets will inevitably lead to greed and corruption where a few will make out financially as bandits, while innocent investors will lose dearly.

The New Deal was responsible for some powerful and important accomplishments. It put people back to work. It saved capitalism. It restored faith in the American economic system, while at the same time it revived a sense of hope in the American people.

The New Deal itself, however, didn't cure the nation's economic woes; World War II did, with a mobilization effort unmatched in our nation's history. But again, we can only speculate what would have happened to our country had the Republicans' zeal for isolationism, which carried the day even after Germany invaded Poland in 1939, prevailed after Japan gave us a wakeup call on December 7, 1941.

Isolationism prevailed even as Germany was building its economy and military strength from 1933 to 1939. Between 1939 and 1941, German forces invaded Poland, Denmark, Norway, France, Luxembourg, the Netherlands, Belgium, Yugoslavia, Greece, and the Soviet Union.

The isolationists were silenced by Pearl Harbor. Without the American entry into World War II, however, it's possible Japan would have consolidated its position of supremacy in East Asia and the war in Europe could have dragged on for far longer than it did, with no guarantee as to the eventual outcome.

At the end of World War II, the Soviet Union occupied Bulgaria, Romania, Hungary, Poland and eastern Germany. Great Britain, the United States, France, and the Soviet Union divided Germany and Berlin into four occupation zones to be administered by the four countries. This, of course, didn't satisfy Russia's Joseph Stalin. The rest is history.

In the mid-1960s, conditions in the country necessitated the passage of the Medicare act, as well as the Civil Rights and Voting Rights Acts.

The Republican Party didn't support the New Deal legislation, never favored Medicare, the Civil Rights Act or the Voting Rights Act; and favored isolationism.

These are the three main prongs of the Republicans' 2022 campaign platform. Each one is built on a myth.

THE SAD STATE OF AMERICAN PRINT JOURNALISM--AND A PERSONAL STORY.

The loss of newspapers over the past several years should be a wakeup call for those who cherish our First Amendment's guarantee of a free press. Democracy depends on an informed citizenry; sadly, with the steady, relentless decline of newspapers, the flow of information designed to educate is reduced.

I have a particular interest in the state of American newspapers. My first professional love was journalism, and it came to me quite by accident.

I always wanted to be a lawyer. I watched Perry Mason on TV in the 1950s and 1960s and was enamored at how he won the case each week. (Of course, I didn't consider how he might have fared on the other four workdays.) Only one thing stopped me: finances.

I knew I would have to work for a while once I earned my bachelor's degree. With no great thought or plan, I applied to the University of Florida College of Education. I was taking political science classes and enjoyed them, so I thought I'd teach American history in high school to earn enough to eventually attend law school.

One of my required classes was American history. This was the only class I received less than a C; I missed that C by one point! Turns out the College of Education didn't accept Ds for graduation, so I would have to re-take that class; however, since it wasn't offered again for another year, I would have to either remain in school (and pay additional tuition and incur a year of living expenses which neither my family nor I had) or go home, find a job and hope I would be re-admitted to the college to take this one class (and incur those additional expenses). In either event, I would have to postpone graduation by one year.

I didn't want to do that, so I searched for a program that would accept that D, and found the School of Journalism. I took the entire news reporter print journalism curriculum over one full year and graduated in August of 1965. I only lost two months from my originally planned graduation day.

Eventually, I took a job at the Palm Beach Post-Times and then the Fort Lauderdale News. As a reporter, I covered the police and court beats. I was fortunate to befriend several judges and other public officials who, upon learning of my interest in law, took me under their wing and wrote letters and made phone calls supporting my application. After about two years as a reporter, I made enough money to attend Florida State University's new law school starting in 1967.

I often remind myself how the entire trajectory of my life might have been different had I gotten that C. I would have remained in education, perhaps never attended law school, wouldn't have moved to Tallahassee, met my wife, had two children, etc. Try recalling something in your life that appeared so insignificant at that time, yet could have changed the course of your life.

Please excuse the aside. Back to the source of my distress.

A recent report on the state of local news from Northwestern's Medill School of Journalism, Media, Integrated Marketing Communications, tells the sad story. The United States continues to lose newspapers at a rate of two per week, further dividing the nation into wealthier, faster growing communities with access to local news, and struggling areas without.

According to this report, between the pre-pandemic months of late 2019 and the end of May 2022, more than 360 newspapers closed. Since 2005, the country has lost more than one-fourth of its newspapers and is on track to lose a third by 2025

Most of the communities that have lost newspapers do not get a print or digital replacement, leaving 70 million residents — or a fifth of the country's population — either living in an area with no local news organizations, or one at risk, with only one local news outlet and very limited access to critical news and information that can inform their everyday decisions and sustain grassroots democracy. About seven percent of the nation's counties, or 211, now have no local newspaper. These areas are called "news deserts," and they are growing.

Surviving newspapers, especially dailies, have cut staff and circulation significantly under financial pressure, reducing their ability to fill the gap when communities lose their local papers. More and more dailies are also dropping seven-day-a-week delivery, as they pursue digital subscribers. Forty of the largest 100 daily newspapers now deliver a print edition six or fewer times a week; 11 deliver two times a week or less.

The cause of this precipitous decline can be summed up in one word: competition. But it's more complicated than that. Television's arrival in the 1950s began the decline of newspapers as most people's source of daily news. In the '50s, I lived in New York City, where its eight-plus million residents had as many as a dozen daily newspapers to choose from. But with mergers, that number dropped to seven. Now, there are four serving about that same number. Accompanying this decline was the decline in the variety of in-depth news information from which the public could choose.

Television was the first blow; the explosion of the Internet in the 1990s was the second, and increased the range of media choices available to the average reader while further cutting into newspapers' dominance as the source of news.

A great boon of this communications explosion was the variety of choices; the downside is that, as we have seen in recent years, the rise of misinformation. There are so many varying avenues of information that it's becoming more and more difficult for the audience to discern fact from fiction, truth from lies, etc. This has given fresh meaning to the old saw that a lie can travel around the world while the truth is putting on its shoes.

This trend shows no signs of abating. Suggestions to try to save what remains include stop living in the past and waiting for the glory of print to return; recognize that the old newspaper business model is dead; stop pretending it is the only industry with a big audience; get serious about classifieds again; and keep the best people.

As a news reporter, I was taught to get the facts and tell the story—the who, what, when, where, why and how. This must remain the polestar of the print journalist.

The major network newscasts each night devote about 21 minutes to actual reporting; advertising takes up the rest. Twenty-four-hour cable news services frequently repeat their newscasts, usually refreshing them as circumstances warrant.

But there is one thing TV news casts, 24-hour news services and radio news can't do—they don't have the time or resources to provide the audience with in-depth reporting.

The kind of detailed, fact-based reporting and accompanying analysis that serves the vital function of fully informing the citizenry can only be accomplished by a newspaper that publishes daily or weekly. (Of course, there are magazines that perform this function; however, the reader must wait a month for that information.)

I fear that if our nation loses the newspaper, we face giving life to the Washington Post's great lament: "Democracy dies in Darkness."

ENDING THE VICIOUS CYCLE OF FEAR TO SUFFERING BEFORE IT'S TOO LATE.

With each passing day, we see candidates for public office, as well as incumbents, stoking the fires of fear—fear that if not elected, horrible things will happen to all of us. Candidates who are touting their records are being drowned out by the evils that will be unleashed if their opponents win.

It's all about fear; fear of what will be unleashed from the bowels of the Earth if "they" win next week and beyond.

The Internet and 24-hour news programs have provided us with an explosion of information that is predominantly designed to educate. Sadly and regrettably, far too much of this information is designed to make us fearful.

It has been said that fear leads to anger, anger leads to hate, hate leads to suffering.

This, however, leaves out a few steps in this downward cycle. Fear leads to anxiety, anxiety leads to anger, anger leads to blame, blame leads to hate, hate leads to scapegoating and suffering.

It is this cycle that we are now in; and unless this cycle is broken, it could well lead to societal changes unlike anything we or our ancestors ever witnessed before as a nation that is almost 250 years old. We need to ask ourselves what kind of nation do we want to leave to our children, grandchildren and beyond. It is that existential.

For many, fear and anxiety affect mental health. If people feel beaten down by a constant barrage of fear-generating information—nuclear war, global warming, monster storms—they may well develop a feeling of helplessness, and we know misery loves company.

Research suggests that people who are struggling emotionally and psychologically may be drawn to conspiracy theories because they provide certainty and security, knowledge that makes them feel unique or superior to others, and improved self-esteem as a result. Online groups devoted to misinformation also give followers a sense of belonging. People who are vulnerable are susceptible to all sorts of things, including misinformation that they accept as fact. The camaraderie in these groups is energizing, and it even helps soothe the pain of ending relationships with loved ones who hold radically different views. Some argue that we must focus on improving people's capacity for critical thinking as a defense against conspiracy theories. While that's a worthy goal, it won't dispel the allure of finding meaning in false beliefs with others who share the same fervent convictions. The simple fact is people need to feel a sense of belonging, and if that sense is derived from conspiracy theories, then so be it.

Republicans arouse fear by saying that Democrats will bring socialism to America; they will take your hard-earned money and give it to those who haven't worked for it; they will take your freedom and regulate your lives; they will raise your taxes and spend your money on foolish things, and on and on.

Democrats arouse fear by saying that Republicans will bring fascism to America; they will give huge financial advantages to big business and cut safety net programs such as social security, Medicare, unemployment compensation; they will deregulate banks, lending institutions and businesses so that your investments will be at risk; they will take away your pensions, and on and on.

It is also said that fear of what might happen is always worse than what can or will happen. Unfortunately, that is of little consolation to those who, being fearful, become anxious.

In May 2018 the American Psychiatric Association released the results of a national survey suggesting that 39 percent of Americans felt more anxious than they did a year ago, primarily about health, safety, finances, politics and relationships. A 2017 report found that 63 percent of Americans were extremely worried about the future of the nation and that 59 percent considered that time the lowest point in U.S. history that they could remember. Such feelings span the political spectrum. A 2018 Pew Research Center survey found that the majority of both Democrats and Republicans felt that "their side" in politics had been losing in recent years on issues they found important.

Fear and anxiety inevitably lead to the search for a scapegoat, which feeds conspiratorial thinking. In general, people have to blame someone for their fears, anxiety and their woes. They will never blame themselves.

The moves from anger to hatred to scapegoating to suffering is usually swift.

The dangerous consequences of the conspiratorial perspective—the idea that people or groups are colluding in hidden ways to produce a particular outcome—have become painfully clear. The belief that the coronavirus pandemic was an elaborate hoax designed to prevent the reelection of Donald Trump incited some Americans to forgo important public health recommendations, costing lives. The gunman who shot and killed 11 people and injured six others in a Pittsburgh synagogue in October 2018 justified his attack by claiming that Jewish people were stealthily supporting illegal immigrants. In 2016 a conspiracy theory positing that high-ranking Democratic Party officials were part of a child sex ring involving several Washington, D.C.–area restaurants incited one believer to fire an assault weapon inside a pizzeria.

Scapegoating is nothing new. The first recorded use of the term "scapegoat" was in reference to the Jewish Day of Atonement and the Judaic practice of exiling a goat in a symbolic casting off of one's sins. Ancient Greeks practiced scapegoating rituals in exceptional times based on the belief that the repudiation of one or two individuals would save the whole community.

History is clear that African-Americans were scapegoated by being segregated away from the ability to pose any kind of real threat to the cultural, social, political and economic dominance of European-Americans in American life before, after and beyond the Civil War.

In the last few years, we've seen immigrants—Latin Americans, Mideasterners, etc.- scapegoated by our political leaders; scapegoating that continues to this day.

In the past several months, we've seen more examples of scapegoating in the form of a rise in antisemitism. Jews have been scapegoated throughout history; no more horrific example was the Holocaust of less than 100 years ago.

Blame "them" because they look or sound different from "us." It's simple—and destructive.

We are now at the precipice of the suffering stage. It doesn't have to be this way. History shows that it's not the majority who lead the charge from fear to suffering; it's usually a relatively small but extremely vocal minority that has seized control of the narrative.

History teaches the horrors of scapegoating; sadly, many don't learn history's lessons.

There are two things that can be done that will go a long way toward cooling the heat.

First, we must realize that, in the words of Winston Churchill, "We are still masters of our fate. We are still captains of our souls." We can control our destiny rather than having events control us. We can act to eliminate the threat of nuclear war; we can act to reduce the conditions causing climate change or global warming; we can act to address other societal issues that plague us.

Second, there was a time when we proudly extolled the virtues of America as the Great Melting Pot, a celebration of our tapestry of different races, colors and values that blended into one. We need to return to that time. Cooler heads and kinder hearts must take control of our nation's narrative. We have it within ourselves to give life to the phrase that we are indeed a nation of laws, not of men—and not the other way around.

And this can't happen soon enough. Hatred is a cancer; kindness is its cure.

THE DEMOCRATS' CAMPAIGN DISCONNECT AND THE REPUBLICANS' NON-EXISTENT PLAN TO FIGHT INFLATION.

This is the essence of the Democrats' problems during the entire midterm campaign; they are focused on horrible things that will happen with a Republican takeover of Congress, instead of providing assurance that they have a specific plan to curb inflation.

Meanwhile, the Republicans, seizing on the Democrats' vulnerability, have been hammering away at the Democrats' handling of the economy.

For the Democrats, there is a disconnect between their campaign theme and what Americans are experiencing just trying to get by day-to-day.

But while the Republicans have been focusing on the nation's economic woes, they have yet to offer any specific plan on how they will fight inflation.

For their plan, House Speaker hopeful Kevin McCarthy said "we will be energy independent, that lower your prices. We'll take away this runaway spending. We'll make America more productive to curve inflation, what the Democrats have brought us.""

This is the Republican plan. Precisely when will we be energy independent? Certainly not anytime soon. As for "runaway spending," there are two questions that haven't been answered: first, what programs will be cut? Social security? Medicare? Any other safety net programs that actually put money into the hands of consumers? Second, how will cutting spending reduce prices, particularly since the energy spike was caused by Russia's war on Ukraine and the supply chain issues caused by the lingering Covid-19 pandemic? And isn't controlling inflation primarily the job of the Federal Reserve? What is the Republican response to that?

And how will Republicans make America more productive? How long will this take?

If cutting spending puts more money into the hands of consumers, won't that cause prices to rise, since people will have more to spend on gas, food, rent, etc.?

Republicans are using their usual core buzzwords, but the devil's in the details--and they haven't given the voters those details. We can only wonder whether they have a real legislative plan to fight inflation. With the election just two days away, it's too late to inform the voters now.

WHERE DO WE GO FROM HERE?

One day before the midterm elections, just about every poll shows the Republicans taking over the House, and they have a solid shot at taking control of the Senate. The campaign is over; I doubt there are any undecideds now.

Republicans certainly have the upper hand on two big issues: the economy and street crime. They also have the two big Ms going for them: momentum and money. All the Democrats seem to have are Biden's legislative record (which requires more effort to explain than just a few emotive words, and the voters' short attention span doesn't help) and fear of a Republican Party beholden to the extreme right wing.

Assuming the polls are accurate (and even if they're not), the question that must now be asked is where do we go from here? We don't have to search far and wide to know what the Republican Party's priorities are; they have been unabashed about their plans. Recalling the quote "vengeance is mine," its leadership has already promised to investigate all of those who dared to challenge Donald Trump and all things Trumpism represents.

Trump and his MAGA loyalists have prepared an enemies list. Those on it include investigators who uncovered evidence of Russian influence in the 2016 presidential election; Republicans who voted to impeach him for seeking dirt on Joe Biden's son-and Joe Biden-in return for the release of appropriated funds; and Republicans who voted to impeach him for inciting a riot on January 6 in furtherance of his lies about a rigged election.

House cronies will also extract revenge on Attorney General Merrick Garland and FBI Director Christopher Wray, and anyone else who had a role in seizing documents unlawfully taken by Trump from the White House and carelessly stowed at his Mar-a-Lago estate.

Not to be left out of Trump's crosshairs, his foot soldiers will also call Dr. Anthony Fauci and anyone else who dared to question Trump's incompetent handling of the COVID pandemic.

Then, to embarrass Biden, they'll call Hunter Biden, who will most likely assert his Fifth Amendment right against self-incrimination.

In short, we'll most likely see a switching-of-sides replay; that is, we can expect from these witnesses what some of Trump's loyalists did when they were subpoenaed: rely on executive privilege or, where lawyers are involved, the attorney-client privilege. Some of those called to testify actually might relish the idea of jousting with the likes of Rep. Jim Jordan or Sen. Ted Cruz or Rand Paul and their ideological colleagues. That will make for great theater.

As for those subpoenaed, assuming they exert a privilege, we can expect another round of seemingly endless court battles similar to what we've seen from Trump and his most ardent loyalists.

Meanwhile, the nation's pressing economic, social and civic problems will go unattended as revenge and the culture wars take priority. While Republicans hammered away at the Democrats' handling of the economy, they never offered a specific plan to deal with rising costs and stagnant wages. If successful at the polls, let's see how fast they come up with one—assuming they come up with one.

The election focus now shifts to the 2024 presidential race and the 800-pound elephant in the room. As a preface to a Donald Trump candidacy (and recognizing the criminal investigations pending against him, with the possibility of more to follow), there is nothing in the Constitution that prohibits a convicted felon from serving as president. The qualifications are clearly set out, and the Supreme Court has been loath to add any additional qualifiers, such as not having been convicted of a felony. Attempts to pass a law prohibiting convicted felons from serving as president would be dead on arrival in a Republican-led Congress.

There is a provision in the Constitution, section 3 of the Fourteenth Amendment, however, that prohibits "an officer of the United States who, having taken an oath to support the Constitution, ""shall have engaged in insurrection or rebellion against the same... ." This provision has been interpreted to prohibit any person who has gone to war against the nation, or given aid and comfort to the nation's enemies, from running for federal or state office unless Congress by a two-thirds vote specifically permits it. This interpretation would not apply to Trump's situation.

The current state of the law, therefore, would allow a convicted felon to run for president.

The reality, however, is that there are those several criminal investigations lurking over Trump, and whatever charges are brought, if any, will be subject to unprecedented litigation for at least the foreseeable future. No president has ever been prosecuted for violation of the criminal law, so the litigation will be intense and of long duration, to say the least.

Assuming Trump runs in 2024 and is successful, there should be no doubt what he will do once he's back in the White House. He has been very vocal about his plans.

Assuming that his congressional loyalists haven't completely exacted their vengeance on Trump's behalf against his enemies over the next two years, he and his congressional followers will press forward.

He will issue pardons to most, if not all, of his "patriots" who took part in the January 6 insurrection at the capital. He will issue pardons to all of his cronies who defied House subpoenas, in addition to those who were convicted of contempt of Congress.

Since the pardon power of a president is unlimited, the number of people he could pardon could reach into the hundreds, perhaps including family members and even himself should he consider it necessary.

Above all, he will demand and command loyalty.

He will purge the entire executive branch of the federal government of the "deep state;" those officials and aides who put their oaths and the Constitution above loyalty to Donald Trump. If members of the "deep state" are protected civil servants, he will force them out or move them to other positions where they pose no threat. There are many forms of punishment he and his obedient followers could dish out to his enemies.

He will fill vacancies with only his most rabid loyalists. Where congressional approval is required and he doesn't believe the Senate will rubber-stamp his nominees, he will appoint people to "acting" positions and keep them there as long as possible. If he faces a recalcitrant Senate, he could possibly move people into "acting" positions under a scenario where he never has to have an appointee face confirmation. This would eviscerate Congress' "advise and consent" role, but for an authoritarian, that is of no consequence. This, of course, is a backup plan; if the Senate is in full agreement with his nominees, Trump will have no trouble appointing whoever he wishes no matter how bereft of qualifications they may be.

With the Supreme Court comfortably controlled by the right wing, and with the three liberal justices, aged 52 to 68, who will presumably serve beyond Trump's term, he will focus on filling the rest of the federal judiciary with like-minded jurists.

He will take on the current state of defamation law, hoping to lower the standards for a successful lawsuit against his avowed "enemies of the people" --the press that he claims vilified and victimized him with "fake news" and "hoaxes" over the years.

He will bend the federal government to his will and pleasure. He will do whatever it takes to ensure that he names his successor.

Internationally, since Trump chose to believe Russian despot Vladimir Putin over his own intelligence community regarding Russia's interference in the 2016 election, there is no reason to believe he will favor our nation's intelligence apparatus in the future, especially as it pertains to Putin. Judging from his past conduct as president, we can expect Trump to continue to diss our allies; end current alliances such as NATO; withdraw our nation from various treaties past administrations believed supported our national interests; and continue to look favorably on authoritarian leaders around the world. In fact, there is every reason to believe he will emulate them.

He will be predisposed to issuing orders or directives that can be quickly carried out by loyal servants.

He might even try to change the Constitution through the constitutional convention method, which involves a convention called by Congress in response to applications from 34 states; 38 states are needed to ratify whatever the convention produces. Under this method, the Constitution could be completely re-written to provide for, among other things, a future of authoritarian presidents serving beyond two four-year terms. There would be no guardrails around this convention to limit what it could accomplish.

Beginning on January 20, 2025, Trump will be unleashed. There will be no one to tell him "no." The loyalists won't dare to question their "stable genius" who "alone can fix it." They'll be no "deep state" protecting our Constitution; the Congress and courts will be most deferential to him. His wish will be their command. The Democrats will be rendered powerless; there will be no checks and balances.

It will be Sinclair Lewis meeting George Orwell meeting Aldous Huxley.

THIS IS THE POT CALLING THE KETTLE BLACK.

Here's a real laugher. Donald Trump called Ron DeSantis sanctimonious, which means making a show of being morally superior to other people. Imagine that! This is the same person who said in 2016: "I am your voice. I alone can fix it. I will restore law and order."

He asked the voters then to put their faith in him. He certainly showed us what he meant by restoring law and order when he incited a riot at the capital on January 6 and earlier this year when he stole classified government records and took them to Mar-a-Lago.

This is a classic example of the pot calling the kettle black; people should not criticize someone else for a fault that they have themselves.

But this is Trump's style: accusing others of the same kind of behavior he exemplifies.

Still, it makes for a good laugh for Trump, of all people, to accuse someone else of moral superiority.

WHO CONTROLS SOCIAL MEDIA CONTENT? NO ONE.

Several comedians have had their Twitter accounts temporarily suspended for impersonating owner Elon Musk. To those who are shouting about the First Amendment's freedom of speech, it's essential to understand this point: the First Amendment applies to government action. Remember the first words of the First Amendment: "Congress shall make no law...abridging the freedom of speech.... ."

Twitter is a social media company that is privately owned, in this case by multibillionaire Musk. He can choose to prohibit, censor or restrict content to his heart's content. He can block anyone at anytime from posting anything he doesn't like. Whether he has a board of directors, line officers, or whatever his business model might be, he has complete authority to decide content.

If you think this is un-American, it isn't. Twitter is his baby and he can treat it as he pleases.

And to make the point further, all social media are privately owned. Google, Facebook, Instagram, Snapchat are all owned by very wealthy people who have full authority to control their respective content.

Of course, these companies are bound by the same rules that most companies must follow, such as generally agreed-upon definitions of fair business practices, truth in advertising, and so on.

In fact, Facebook was heavily fined for failure to comply with rules set by the FTC.

What is important here is that Facebook wasn't fined because the company violated its social media regulations — there aren't any.

So, if you don't like Musk controlling Twitter's content--or any of the social media billionaires who run their companies with an iron hand--you can buy the company the way Musk bought Twitter.

Just don't expect Congress, federal regulators or the states to try to control social media content. That pesky First Amendment will get in the way.

We can hope for some way to eliminate misinformation on social media. But if there is going to be some semblance of standards governing social media content, it will be up to the owners to provide those standards, and prevent posting of misinformation, baseless conspiracy theories, and other nonsense that adds nothing that is of benefit to our society.

NO RED WAVE, BUT THE PROMISE OF A BATTLE ROYAL IN FLORIDA AS THE PARTIES GAIN THEIR FOOTING.

The Republican Party's hopes for a red wave sweeping a significant majority into both houses of Congress didn't materialize. Now, it looks as if House Republicans will have about a 10-15 vote majority; the Senate looks to be as close for the Republicans as it was under the Democrats. This outcome means the party can't lose too many peel-offs on critical votes.

Republicans focused on the economy, crime and immigration. Democrats focused on abortion and the right wing threat to democracy. It seems the voters focused on all of above, with a message to govern, not toss verbal bombs at one another.

But while the pundits wax on what House Republicans will do over the next few months, there is something that portends a battle royal in Florida going forward and commanding the public's attention.

That is the battle between Florida's two Republican titans, Donald Trump and Ron DeSantis.

I'll deal with that one first.

DeSantis won his re-election bid overwhelmingly. He is young, attractive, well-educated and obviously delivered a message that resonated with the state voters. Trump is the much older former president who was exiled by the voters in 2020 in a fair election, no matter what he and his fellow deniers say.

DeSantis' sin in Trump's mind is that he backed Colorado senate candidate Joe O'Dea, who vowed to campaign against Trump. That's a big no-no in Trumpland. Trump accused O'Dea of being a RINO (Republican In Name Only) and said "Maga Doesn't vote for stupid people with big mouths." (You may add your own comment now. Mine is "yes they do.") That O'Dea lost to incumbent Michael Bennet probably lessens O'Dea's influence going forward to 2024.

Trump has already threatened DeSantis with spreading dirt he claims to have on the governor, saying publicly that he knows more about DeSantis than anyone, except maybe the governor's wife. (I wonder if Trump will call a foreign president for dirt on DeSantis. He's called a foreign leader for dirt on an opponent before.)

DeSantis has just completed his campaign for re-election portraying strength by touting his ability to stand up to bullies and naysayers. Does Trump really believe his threat of slinging mud on DeSantis will dissuade him?

Besides, Trump has his own problems to deal with. By the time he makes his "big" re-election announcement, he may well be facing federal charges arising out of the January 6 attack on the capital and his unlawful removal of classified documents.

Trump, however, believes his base will support him no matter what charges he faces, or what he does. Remember, he said he could shoot someone on a public street and his supporters will still stand with him. The question, of course, is how many MAGA supporters are there who won't shift to another candidate with a better chance of winning in 2024.

For Trump, however, such bloviation or braggadocio is nothing new. He knows more about the military than the generals; more about dictators than anyone else, and on and on. He's the smartest person in government and just about the best president ever; just ask him.

DeSantis knows that the way to stand up to a bully is to stand up to a bully.

And DeSantis might have the support--albeit silent or tepid, at least in the beginning-- of Republican leaders in Congress and in many states who are tired of Trump. Note that Trump's endorsements resulted in a mixed bag. He had some victories, but took some losses--and that's not good for someone who must show invulnerability to be successful.

In short, DeSantis won't be intimidated by someone who had the presidency and didn't know how to keep it. If he's smart—and he is—he'll treat Trump like a hurricane—letting him blow loud and long to his red hats until eventually he blows himself out. DeSantis knows that's how you handle a windbag.

So, gazing into the crystal ball, what can we expect going forward? Certainly another Trump candidacy. There will be some political cannibalization between Trump and DeSantis because in politics, timing is everything and if he doesn't go for the nomination in 2024, his time might have come and gone. Remember, in 2028, DeSantis will be out of the governor's office for two years, and if Trump is elected, he certainly won't do anything to favor DeSantis—unless DeSantis is willing to grovel. And even then, Trump views that as a sign of weakness. If DeSantis is going to make a run for the White House, he must do it now, particularly when Trump has excess baggage, is excess baggage to the party, and Biden is viewed as old and weak.

And then, there are those criminal investigations. The Department of Justice is now in the put-up or shut-up phase; indictments will have to be forthcoming even while Trump is a candidate. I doubt DOJ wants to show timidity while Trump is traveling around the country ranting and raving about his poor treatment by his enemies for the next two years. He'll continue his pity party while lambasting Democrats and those Republicans who remain a thorn in his side.

While Trump and DeSantis try to devour each other, what will the Congressional Republicans be doing?

From what Kevin McCarthy said, the first order of business will be the border. That will, of course, take legislation, which requires Biden's approval. Under Biden's worst case scenario, he has two pens: veto and pardon.

We can expect vigorous investigations into the Biden Administration. They might even impeach Biden knowing there'll be no Senate conviction, just because the House Democrats (and a few Republicans) twice impeached Donald Trump. Of course, there's that little matter of "high crimes and misdemeanors" required by the Constitution to justify impeachment, but you can bet the House Republicans won't have a problem with that: they'll just use whatever minuscule scraps they find, expand them to self-serving ends, and smack the constitutional requirement onto their pre-conceived result.

As the House Republicans flex their muscles, they might even work out a devil's bargain with Biden: sign all legislation they pass, or they'll impeach him for nonfeasance (translation: not doing the job of president by not approving their legislation. How dare Biden veto their legislation!).

Knowing Biden's demeanor over 36 years in the senate, eight years as vice president and two as president, he will no doubt tell House Republicans where they can put that so-called bargain.

The Republicans, faced with the perceived need to save face, will raise a hue and cry and might just impeach him no matter what, leaving it to history to explain that while Trump was impeached for violating federal law (first, by seeking dirt on Biden from a foreign country in return for release of appropriated funds; and second, by using a lie to instigate an insurrectionist attack on the capital), Biden was impeached solely to exact revenge.

And if those investigations get hot and heavy, Biden won't hesitate to use his pardon pen.

The message sent by the voters is that both parties must get off the outrage train and deal with real issues that affect real people. The battle should be over which party can better deliver the goods to the voters. Unfortunately, lessons taught are not necessarily learned.

Considering the campaign rhetoric, Republicans now have the burden of showing they can do a better job at governing than the Democrats. But here is their problem: we know how well they governed during Trump's four years; that's why the Democrats took over Congress in the 2018 midterm and 2020 elections, and why they ousted Trump in 2020. Remember the wonderful job Trump did with the COVID pandemic? The voters certainly did. Whether they like it or not, Republicans are going to have to deal with the baggage that is Trump.

As for Biden, I think many voters expected him to be the political version of "Mr. Excitement," the name given to the late singer Jackie Wilson. But policy wonk Biden was never the type of person to arouse great emotion with a stem-winding speech.

He didn't serve himself well by withdrawing from Afghanistan, and even after the Democrats had a numerical majority in the Senate following the 2020 election, I doubt Biden and his team expected two senators—Joe Manchin and Kyrsten Sinema—to play hardball with fellow Democrats.

Biden will start next year being the first 80-year-old president. In 2024, he'll be 82. Of course, he's going to say he'll run again; he doesn't want to become a lame duck for two years. But reality makes it unlikely he'll seek another term. He doesn't need it; he's already accomplished his greatest goal. He had a reasonably good record of legislative success his first two years. He knows with a Republican Congress, or even a Republican House, his grand agenda is dashed.

Meanwhile, the Democrats have a couple of rising heavyweights in Govs. Gavin Newsom of California, J. B. Pritzker of Illinois, Gretchen Whitmer of Michigan and Kathy Hochul of New York, and Sens. Jon Ossoff and Tammy Duckworth, just to name a few.

Both parties will have to find their footing beginning next January, while the Republican Party heavyweights take shots at each other. All with an eye on 2024.

Ain't politics fun?

AS THE DUST SETTLES, SPECULATION ABOUNDS.

American politics knows no off-season. As the dust continues to settle over the November elections, speculation abounds as we move toward the 2024.

But first things first. Control of the senate once again looks like it will come down to the Georgia runoff next month between incumbent Democrat Raphael Warnock and Republican Herschel Walker. The current count in all decided races is 48 Democrats and 49 Republicans. In Nevada, the Republican candidate is ahead of the Democratic incumbent; in Arizona, the Democratic incumbent is ahead. If those totals hold, Republicans will have 50, Democrats 49. However, if the Democrats pick up Georgia, the party will once again have the tiebreaker in the vice president. Recall that two years ago, control of the senate boiled down to Georgia's two senate seats, both won by Democrats over incumbent Republicans.

Regardless of the eventual outcome in the senate, neither party will have any wiggle room; both parties will need complete unanimity to pass just about anything. Expect plenty of wheeling-and-dealing in the upper chamber of Congress, in particular over presidential appointments, particularly for the judiciary and changes to cabinet officers.

It's becoming clear that the Republicans will take control of the House of Representatives. This will stymie Joe Biden's legislative program even with the amount of horse-trading that will highlight the next two years. Remember that before we get to 2024, we have to navigate 2023.

Both Biden and House Republicans want to proceed with their respective agendas—however far apart each may be—and there will plenty of give-and-take as both try to make their respective cases for the big three issues—inflation, street crime and immigration. There will be proposals, counter-proposals, threats, intimidation, backing off, cooler heads—at least let's hope so.

Policy is detail-driven, and the public's attention span isn't particularly geared to the nuances of policy detail.

But what will garner the public's attention is the amount of verbal blasts that will feature the Donald Trump-Ron DeSantis war.

Trump wants to announce his bid to return to the White House as early as next week. He no doubt is trying to upstage DeSantis' huge victory while beating any announcement of criminal charges against him by the Department of Justice.

But after the Republican Party's anticipated red wave was dashed, party leaders are leveling their frustration at Trump, believing his baggage weighed down some of their candidates. Trump is facing a new form of criticism—from his own loyalists who nevertheless put party above him.

Trump is therefore having to defend himself against charges by members of his own party, even as he must deal with DeSantis and the Department of Justice.

Pundits have chimed in earlier, saying Trump is in charge so long as he appears invulnerable; but as soon as that shield disappears, he will be attacked from all sides with vengeance. Remember, politics is survival of the fittest, and right now, Trump as the fittest is taking a big hit.

DeSantis meanwhile needs to say nothing. He can quietly move his chess pieces into proper position for 2024, ignoring Trump's silly name-calling ("Ron De-Sanctimonious") and threats of revealing dirt on him. Moreover, DeSantis needs to do nothing directed at Trump; he can leave that for the party leadership in Congress, and the criminal justice system.

DeSantis is in the catbird seat, and Trump has to know this. DeSantis also has an advantage knowing Trump is an emotional, mercurial person known for putting his mouth in motion before his brain is in gear. DeSantis would be wise to let Trump twist slowly in the wind, making one loud bleat after another, and continue to test the tolerance level of congressional Republicans and even some MAGAites who have Trump fatigue and would have no trouble shifting loyalties.

What about Joe Biden? My take is he won't run again unless he is confident Trump will be his opponent. Biden believes—as he did in 2020—that he is the only Democrat who can beat him. For Trump to have the inside track to the nomination, he will have had to stop DeSantis and come out ahead of the Department of Justice—two huge tasks. Biden also knows Trump never received the popular vote; Clinton beat him by 2.9 million votes, and Biden himself beat him by around 8 million.

We know Trump abhors losing. If he believes he can't be nominated either as a result of DeSantis' strength, the criminal charges, or both, you can bet the mortgage Trump will withdraw, blast everyone (but himself) for his woes, and even threaten to take the party down with him, pretty much in the same manner as he did with the two Georgia senate seats two years ago.

For Trump, it's not about party loyalty, it's about him. And if he can't have the White House, he's not going to be too keen on someone else (translation: DeSantis) snatching it from him.

With Trump out of the picture, what might Biden do? Assuming DeSantis is the party's standard bearer, he will be 45. He's handsome, has a beautiful family and a tremendous amount of goodwill. And he's not Donald Trump won't have the Trump baggage. That he's anathema to the Democrats is of no consequence; any Republican will be anathema to the Democrats.

Biden, on the other hand, will be 82. The physical contrast between the two couldn't be more profound. But Biden doesn't want to be a lame duck president any longer than absolutely necessary.

With his legislative program pretty much DOA; with the prospects of facing a younger, more vibrant candidate; facing the rigors of a presidential campaign that is taxing on candidates anyway; and with his few legislative accomplishments already of record, he could well walk away sometime around March of 2024—similar to what Lyndon Johnson did in 1968. He achieved his ultimate goal; there are no more mountains to conquer. He said he would be a transitional president; he could go out as a king- or queenmaker.

Of course, party officials will want him to make his decision clear as early as possible to give candidates the maximum opportunity to get their names out before the public. However, there are party leaders whose names are fairly well-known, so name recognition might not be so essential as to make Biden announce his intentions any earlier than he wants to.

If not Biden, then who for the Democrats? VP Kamala Harris is tied closely to Biden, hasn't shown much strength independent of him, really can't do that anyway, and has her own limited baggage to deal with. In addition, the party (and its supporters) may be looking for a complete break from Biden, and that includes Harris. She really can't do anything until Biden makes his decision. He holds the cards.

The history of the past few vice presidents show that they are inextricably tied to the president's popularity. Hubert Humphrey suffered greatly because of Johnson's unpopularity over Vietnam. Gerald Ford suffered greatly because of his pardon of Richard Nixon. Bush I benefitted from Ronald Reagan's enormous popularity. Biden himself dealt with personal issues and took time off before running in 2020. Harris' fortunes would depend on Biden's popularity, and right now, that's not a good bet for her.

I have already offered some names as Democratic hopefuls. They are primarily governors from large states.

My personal choice is the same person I mentioned during Biden's consideration of a running mate. I think Gov. Gretchen Whitmer of Michigan would be a formidable candidate. While the party has other strong candidates, Whitmer would be the poster person for all things wrong with right wing politics. She was threatened, stood up to her assailants, and won re-election. Every time DeSantis mentions his anti-Woke legislation, Whitmer's presence will be a constant reminder of what right wing did extremism did to her. DeSantis would be forced to either accept to reject Trumpism—not a comfortable thing for him either way.

But it's all speculation.

A SUBTLE MESSAGE TO REPUBLICANS: PROCEED AT YOUR OWN RISK

We know the anticipated Republican Party red wave ran into a Democratic wall. Going into the midterm elections, Republicans had every advantage going for them. An unpopular opposition party president; historical losses for the incumbent party; the core issues of inflation, street crime and immigration; weak Democratic messaging, etc.

And yet, with every advantage, at best, the Republicans will have the barest of majorities in the senate, and a relatively slim majority in the House.

Before the election, Republican House leadership was planning to investigate the Biden Administration for everything from the Afghanistan withdrawal COVID to the January 6 investigation to the FBI raid at Mar-a-Lago. Biden was weak and vulnerable. This was supposed to be how the party was going to exact revenge for its leader, the strong and powerful Donald Trump.

But a funny thing happened on their way to that forum. Now, Biden doesn't look so weak. He survived the usual party losses and is taking a victory lap. It's Trump who took a beating and is being blamed for his party's failure to realize that hoped-for red wave. This is a classic reversal of fortune that was unexpected for both parties.

Now, it's up to the congressional Republicans to deal with inflation, street crime and immigration. While they were strong on the rhetoric, they have yet to offer a plan to address each of these issues.

The voters sent an unmistakable message the other day: deal with these issues, and cut the extremism.

Where is the Republican Party's plan to ease the consumer's burden? If it's cutting taxes, how will they raise the revenue needed to run the government and fund the programs? If it's cutting programs, which programs will they want to strip from the voters?

As for dealing with street crime, will they seek more law enforcement officers; provide intervention programs; or employment programs? Each of these costs money. Where will it come from?

Every program costs money that must be raised by tax revenue. If Republicans are consistent, they will want to continue—perhaps increase—tax benefits to the wealthy. This leaves the burden of raising revenue squarely on the shoulders of the middle class.

The biggest government costs are the social service programs—the ones that benefit the greatest number of Americans. Do they want to take an ax to social security, Medicare, and the other programs that are the bedrock of our nation?

I doubt middle class voters would be pleased.

And if they decide to cut programs, this will force Biden's hand—the one holding the veto pen—which in turn would allow him to seize the upper hand by branding the Republicans as anti-middle class.

Tax breaks for the wealthy raises huge amounts of campaign funds, but a billionaire still has one vote, the same as everyone elsc.

While addressing these profound issues, do the Republicans want to carry forth on their plans to investigate the Democrats ad nauseam, impeach Biden, perhaps impeach Attorney General Merrick Garland, FBI Director Christopher Wray, and others?

The purpose of these investigations was to vindicate Trump. But now, with a materially weakened former president about to face criminal charges and being vilified by party leadership for the party's losses, do the congressional Republicans want to spend so much capital on vindicating someone who's now extremely vulnerable and may not be the key player going forward? Or would it be more prudent to show real leadership by addressing these substantive issues, giving Trump some lip service while letting him fend for himself?

As the voters wait for economic relief, safer communities and a stemming of the influx of immigrants, does the House leadership want to expend the time and resources on investigative and impeachment proceedings, especially if the evidence is scant or largely manufactured? And more important politically, does the leadership want to risk making Biden a martyr going into 2024?

And does the leadership want to do this after the voters told them in no uncertain terms to cut the extremism and solve the problems?

Will the House Republican extremists who want to investigate and impeach at all costs force the leadership to moderate?

The voters made it clear that Republicans will proceed with their pre-election promises at their own risk. Stay tuned for an eventful 2023.

POLITICS IS A BLOOD SPORT. JUST LOOK AT THE BATTLE BETWEEN TRUMP AND DESANTIS.

"Politics is war without bloodshed." This quote from Mao Tse Tung is on target, although politics played a large role in the blood spilled on January 6, and the attacks since then.

Proof that politics is a blood sport is the war being waged within the Republican Party between former president Donald Trump and Florida Gov. Ron DeSantis, viewed by Trump as his biggest obstacle to his party's nomination in 2024.

Trump is trying every which way to snare DeSantis in a war of words. Trump, who is now a weakened public figure due to his party's less than expected showing in the midterm elections, knows he must remove all possible opponents if he's to have any chance of getting his party's nomination in 2024.

Ron DeSantis is Exhibit A, and Trump will use loyalty, intimidation and threats—even threats of violence—to remove DeSantis from his path to the nomination and the White House.

Trump has branded DeSantis with the type of description he's used successfully against other opponents like Jeb Bush ("low energy"), Ted Cruz ("lyin' Ted"), Marco Rubio ("little Marco"), etc. He thinks this is cute, and his MAGA folks swallow it like honey.

For DeSantis, it's "Ron De-sanctimonious." It doesn't matter whether his MAGAs know what sanctimonious means; Trump makes the point and his loyal servants get a good laugh.

This worked effectively in 2016. But back then, Trump was viewed as a successful businessman with a populist message, while his opponents treated him as an outlier who knew nothing about politics. His television persona only added to his image and generated such a level of curiosity that the media gave him large amounts of free publicity.

There was some noise about stiffing contractors, how he treated women ("locker room talk") and payoffs for his affairs, but that was treated as nothing more than noise; it did nothing to tarnish his image as an eminently successful businessman and showman or impresario.

But that was then; going forward to 2024 will be vastly different because of how much we learned about the real Donald Trump.

We know his image as an eminently successful businessman has taken a big hit. The many lawsuits by contractors who were stiffed by him; his failure to disclose his tax returns for fear of disclosing how much he's really worth; and on and on, essentially removes the image that voters had six years ago.

His handling of the first major crisis of his presidency, COVID, revealed him to be more of a bumbler than an effective leader. He was lambasted and made to appear the fool for suggesting that COVID victims ingest bleach to cure the virus.

Although Trump developed a reputation for lying or, to put it more gently, engaging in exaggeration, his true penchant for lying was revealed after he lost his re-election bid in 2020. His actions in fomenting an insurrection at the capital, which took five lives and several others in the aftermath, including suicide by law enforcement officers, showed that it was about him, not the country or his party.

The lying continues to this day.

Considering that Trump is attacking everyone who he believes might pose a threat to him going forward (such as Virginia Gov. Glenn Youngkin), it is a legitimate question for Republicans to ask whether Trump will destroy the party rather than lose to any other candidate. We know he's attacked Mitch McConnell, Kevin McCarthy, and others too lengthy to list here. We know he's blaming everyone but himself for the election losses. How much more of Trump will the party leaders take?

Just the other day, retiring Rep. Mo Brooks of Alabama, who at one time was one of Trump's most vocal supporters, called Trump "dishonest, disloyal, incompetent, crude." Brooks pledged complete loyalty to Trump, only to have Trump toss him under the bus. This should serve notice to all of Trump's congressional loyalists that he will dump them if he finds it convenient. Loyalty for Trump is a one-way street.

Trump could get by with his poor treatment of others because of how powerful he was with his MAGA crowd, and the perception of Trump as a consummate winner.

That perception doesn't square with reality. In 2018, he lost the House of Representatives. In 2020, he lost the presidency and the senate. In 2022, his election deniers suffered great losses; in fact, all of his secretary of state candidates in the key battleground states Trump hoped would elect him in 2024 were soundly defeated.

With everything lined up for the Republicans this election cycle, the party suffered major losses not only in Congress, but in state governorships and legislatures as well.

This is a record of losses by a president/former president that is unparalleled in recent history.

We should expect more congressional loyalists and his MAGA manics to peel off from him as they come to realize this emperor has no clothes.

Trump knows he must now run on what the public knows about him. In two presidential campaigns, he never received a majority of the popular vote. Does he really believe he will get that in 2024? He's banking on the electoral college vote, but even that will be tenuous since he lost to Biden by the same vote he beat Clinton. And we've learned a lot more about Trump since 2020—all negative stuff.

This is why his only path to his party's nomination is to remove all obstacles that stand in his way, and he will try to do this the only way he knows how: by first appealing to loyalty and, failing of that, by intimidation and attacks and, failing of that, by arousing his base (whatever may be left of it) to such a degree that his opponents fear violence.

DeSantis knows this. He knows that by not responding in kind, he's only frustrating and angering Trump that much more. Trump needs a willing opponent, but DeSantis knows that when you're ahead, you don't need to do a thing.

It has been said that the opposite of hate is not love; it's indifference. This is the one thing Trump can't handle. He needs someone to match him blast for blast. Indifference--ignoring him--only makes his that much angrier.

The second thing he can't handle is being mocked or laughed at. Sooner rather than later, his "enemies" will begin to laugh at his bluster, treating Trump like a buffoon. You can only imagine how this will affect him.

DeSantis has the momentum and a path to the high road. He knows that Trump's MAGA base has nowhere else to go if Trump is removed as a viable candidate. Trump may tell them not to vote—as he did in the Georgia senate races two years ago—but whether they will continue to follow him down that road is iffy. After all, I doubt they would want a Democrat in the White House after the 2024 election.

As for Trump's congressional loyalists, DeSantis knows the only place they'll go with Trump out of the picture is with the strongest remaining candidate—him. (Or perhaps someone else, but not Trump.) In essence, these Trump loyalists will become party loyalists, which is exactly what DeSantis and the party leaders want. The Republican Party simply doesn't want a Democrat in the White House. If DeSantis is viewed as the one who can prevent that, the party leaders, loyalists and supporters will fall in line.

It won't be about Trump anymore. And that's fine with the party. There remains only when the party will have had enough of him.

THE ANSWER TO THE VOTERS' "RIGGED ELECTION" REJECTION IS REPUBLICAN PARTY TONE-DEAFNESS.

The Republican Party took it on the chin in the November midterm elections. That's putting it mildly, considering historical trends that tell us the party in the White House suffers significant losses in Congress in these midterm elections.

Bowing to Donald Trump's false "rigged election" claim that led to a violent and deadly insurrection at our nation's Capital, 19 states parroted the sudden need to deal with non-existent voter fraud by enacting over 30 laws designed to make voting more difficult for Democrats and easier for Republicans.

These post-2020 laws driven by the Republican Party in lockstep with Trump's known lie include:

Shortening the time to apply for and deliver a mail ballot; making it harder to remain on absentee voting lists; eliminating or limiting sending mail ballot applications and mail ballots to voters who don't request them; restricting assistance in returning a voter's mail ballot; restricting the number of mail ballot drop boxes; imposing stricter signature requirements for mail ballots; imposing harsher voter ID requirements; expanding voter purges or risk faulty voter purges; increasing barriers for voters with disabilities; banning snacks and water to voters waiting in line; eliminating election day registration; reducing the number of polling places, and hours of operation; increasing the number of voters for each precinct; and limiting early voting days or hours.

Together with these targeted voting restrictions, the Republicans had the issues of inflation, crime, and immigration driving their message. And they had an unpopular Democratic president viewed as being out of touch, incompetent and senile they blamed for the nation's woes. The only thing going for Democrats was a Democracy vs. fascism warning that the polls said wasn't resonating with the voters. The Republicans had their message; the Democrats seemed incapable of finding their voice. The Republicans appeared strong; the Democrats weak.

And then the voters spoke in no uncertain terms.

Stop the lying. Stop the nonsense of conspiracy theories. Stop offering candidates more suited for mental institutions than for public office. And most of all, stop the culture war and work on programs and policies that address the real problems that affect real people.

No more "rigged election" excuses.

Now, as the election moves into the rear view mirror, it isn't the Democrats who are engaging in the blame game; it's the Republicans who are doing the finger-pointing, looking for that mysterious scapegoat. This has all the appearance of internal blood-letting—which of course the Democrats won't try to prevent.

Republicans would do well to recall William Shakespeare's quote from "Julius Caesar"-- "The fault lies not in our stars, but in ourselves." They could also take heed of Walt Kelly's famous comic strip "Pogo" where he said: "We have met the enemy and he is us."

Donald Trump is not the Democratic Party's fault. He was chosen by Republican voters eventually forged by the party leadership. The Democrats didn't force Republicans to turn a blind ear to Trump's incessant lying and kowtow to wacky conspiracy theories and right wing extremist groups. This is fully on the Republican Party.

Nevertheless, showing how tone deaf the Republican Party is, no less a Trump supporter than Missouri Sen. Josh Hawley has gone on record as saying the traditional old Republican Party, the GOP, is dead. You might recall Hawley from January 6 fame (or rather infamy) where he is shown fist-pumping the insurrectionists attacking the capital, only to be seen a bit later fleeing from the capital as the rioters closed in.

Hawley said the party must get out in front of the issues, and proceeded to wax the mantra of inflation, crime and immigration—the issues that failed to move the voters to the Republican Party in the recently concluded election.

It's not clear who exactly Hawley sees as part of "the old party," but he has made it clear that he doesn't side with Senate Minority Leader Mitch McConnell.

Hawley said the party leadership was responsible for the party's midterm failures. He singled out McConnell, saying he would not vote for the Kentucky senator to be the party leader regardless of which party wins the Senate. He was also the first senator to publicly break ranks with McConnell in 2020 when he announced his plan to object to the 2020 election results.

Pointedly, he made no mention of Trump, who endorsed extreme, unlikeable and unqualified candidates in several states, forcing better qualified candidates to the sidelines. All those election deniers and voting fraud frauds were soundly rejected by the voters. Yet, Hawley blames McConnell who dared not tell Trump (at least publicly) that he was backing a host of losers.

The prospect of an avowed election denier seeking to become a leading spokesperson for the party's future after the drubbing it took is a classic example of tone-deafness.

As for McConnell, he could now be facing a challenge to his leadership position, including from Florida Sen. Rick Scott, the chairman of the GOP's campaign arm. Trump, too, is calling on political allies to oust McConnell and is condemning him for the party's weak and disappointing midterm results.

Hawley has visions of greater things for himself: he in the process of forging his own path in the Senate with other Trump Republicans. During the midterms, he backed JD Vance, a fellow Trump-backed successful Ohio senate candidate.

Hawley also supported Blake Masters in Arizona. Democratic candidate Mark Kelly defeated Masters, handing the Republicans a crucial loss and helping the Democratic Party retain its majority in the upper chamber. Hawley is focusing on the comparatively few Republican victories, instead of the massive number of losses, including all election-denying secretary of state candidates in battleground states.

The bottom line here is that, after the Republican Party's thumping at the polls—rejecting extremists and conspiracy theorists--Hawley believes the party's future lies in the hands of those extremists, conspiracy theorists and wild-eyed flamethrowers just substantially rejected by the voters.

The Democrats have be elated at this graphic example of political self-immolation.

DO THE HOUSE REPUBLICANS HAVE A POLITICAL DEATH WISH?

Here is a candidate for the loudest, longest laugh of the day. As Dave Barry says, you can't make up this stuff.

Florida Rep. Matt Gaetz, fresh off his successful re-election bid, said, in opposing Kevin McCarthy for speaker of the house: "With a slim majority, we shouldn't be starting the C team. We need to put our star players in a position to shine brightest so that we can attract more people to our policies and ideas."

Let's see. Gaetz, one of Donald Trump's truest of true believers, thinks McCarthy is a member of the C team and doesn't want him as speaker. Rather, the Republicans should choose someone from the party's A team -- one of their "star players" probably on the order of Jim Jordan, Marjorie Taylor Greene or Lauren Boebert--or some other election denier and conspiracy theory proponent--to be house speaker. To Gaetz, the best and the brightest among the house Republicans are made up of these mental giants. Of course, Gaetz fancies himself as one as well.

Didn't the voters just reject election deniers and conspiracy theorists endorsed by Donald Trump and his loyalists? I'm sure those voters would love to hear about the "policies and ideas" emanating from this crew---the "policies and ideas" just roundly tossed in the garbage can on election day.

Maybe these folks on the extreme right wing have a political death wish. Perhaps they like the idea of losing elections by showing again how they can be too extreme for the voters' general taste.

The members of this motley crew might fancy themselves as mental giants. I find the word "gnats" more appropriate.

THE REPUBLICAN "PLAN" TO FIGHT CRIME:
THE DEVIL'S IN THE DETAILS.

House Republican leader Kevin McCarthy let slip his party's plan to fight crime---put 100,000 more officers on the street. Sounds simple enough. Gets the party faithful nodding their heads in support.

But as it is said, the devil's in the details. What McCarthy and his backers don't want the public to consider are those details (assuming they have them), so I'll take a stab (no pun intended) at it.

At the outset, McCarthy is talking about street crime. Robberies, assaults, murders—the crimes that get the public's attention.

He's not talking about the white-collar, corporate boardroom crime that siphon off billions of dollars that could make their way into the federal treasury to be spent on programs designed to fight street crime.

We know Republicans love to give huge tax breaks to the mega-wealthy corporate big-shots in return for campaign donations and other quid pro quo benefits not available to the middle class.

So, let's do some basic math. Hiring 100,000 cops at an average salary of $50,000 each per year adds up to $5 billion. But that's just the start. Added to that annual amount are pension and workers' compensation funds.

Then, each cop has to be properly outfitted with crime-fighting equipment (uniforms, guns, tasers, handcuffs, walkie-talkies, etc.). Facilities will have to be upgraded to handle these new recruits and additional equipment will have to be purchased, such as cars, etc.

A conservative estimate for start-up costs will reach $10-12 billion.

White collar crime and corporate tax breaks take billions of dollars that would otherwise go to the treasury. So, while the treasury funds are reduced due to the confluence of corporate crimes and tax breaks, McCarthy and his fellow Republicans have to come up with this $10-12 billion in new money. And again, that's just the first year. To maintain this 100,000-person presence on the streets will necessitate annual funding of at least half that amount each year (since presumably it won't be necessary to completely outfit each officer with new equipment every year).

As the treasury is depleted by billions of dollars, and billions of dollars must go toward this crime-fighting effort, the question naturally arises: where will this new money come from?

To put it bluntly, as the treasury is reduced by billions, billions must be found to fund McCarthy's plan.

We know each program passed by Congress costs money. To make up for this reduction, programs will have to be cut.

We also know Republicans abhor social programs. They believe these programs are examples of wasteful spending, provide handouts to the lazy, and do nothing to promote individual initiative and self-motivation. (How these concerns might apply to those corporate tax breaks is never mentioned.)

But considering the Republican mentality here, it should be obvious that to fund these 100,000 cops, programs will have to be cut.

Those programs that could face the ax may well be those that are specifically targeted to deal with street crime. Intervention programs. After-school programs. Jobs programs. In general, the ax may fall on those programs designed to deal with idle time by providing safe and healthy places for groups to gather for meaningful social activities, work, and to generally avoid the vicious cycle that leads to crime.

They may also sharpen the ax with an eye toward larger funding sources, such as social security, Medicare and other social network programs. Of course, reducing family income for the most vulnerable and needy has its own risks to our nation's well-being, but that's a matter that recalls the devil-details quote.

We also know Republicans love to cut taxes, but not uniformly. In 2017, they provided permanent tax cuts for the wealthy and tax cuts for the middle class that expire in 2025.

If the Republicans are of a mind not to cut programs, the only viable alternative is to raise taxes. The easiest way to do this is to let those middle class tax cuts expire, or advance the expiration date to next year.

Or they can raise new taxes on the middle class. Or they can do a blending of some program reduction coupled with some increase in taxes...for the middle class.

I wonder if the middle class head-nodders will still support McCarthy's flip crime fighting solution once they realize the details?

WELCOME TO THE WACKY WORLD OF THE "NEW" REPUBLICAN PARTY

Sen. Rick Scott is challenging Mitch McConnell for senate Republican Party leader, blaming McConnell for the party's stunning losses in the recently concluded midterm elections.

Let's see now. Scott served as chairman of the National Republican Senatorial Committee during the current cycle and barnstormed the country in support of some of the party's most high-profile candidates. He doled out millions to party candidates, many of whom were election deniers and Trump loyalists, as is Scott. The voters soundly rejected those candidates.

So, if Scott supported Trump-endorsed candidates, actually helped finance their campaigns, and those candidates lost, then logic dictates that Scott and Trump must share the blame.

But not so fast for the Republican Party. You see, Scott, in taking a page from Trump's playbook of deny and deflect, is blaming McConnell because it's his fault Republican voters didn't turn out in large enough numbers to win. Scott is saying that the Republican voters are there ready, willing and able to support everything that is Trump—including lies, denials, BS and nonsense—but McConnell didn't get them to turn out on election day.

I guess Scott thinks Trump would have won the popular vote in 2016 as well as 2020 had there been a better Republican voter turnout. I guess Scott also thinks his party wouldn't have lost the House of Representatives in 2018, the presidency and Senate in 2020 and the Senate in 2022 had McConnell done a better job getting out the Republican voters. Or perhaps anyone else he can blame for his party's losses.

For Scott, none of these repeated losses can be blamed on Trump's lies, election denials and conspiracy nonsense. And none of these losses can be blamed on Scott for how he campaigned for these losing candidates or how he managed the money flowing to senate candidates endorsed by Trump.

Sen. Josh Hawley says the old Republican Party is "dead." If so, then, welcome to the wacky world of the "new" Republican Party.

EIGHT BILLION PEOPLE.

The United Nations has announced that the world's population has reached eight billion, having doubled from four billion just 48 years ago. But while the world population has grown exponentially, the size of the planet hasn't; as a result, the human race is demanding that the planet continue to provide for a population that will continue to grow.

The United States isn't immune from this population explosion. Fifty years ago, the nation's population was around 203 million. In 2020, that number grew to over 331 million. It is estimated that our nation is adding between two-to-three million each year—and that, too, is expected to increase.

Population numbers don't increase arithmetically; they increase geometrically. This means that if the world population doubled in the last 50 years or so, we can expect that number of eight billion to double over the next 25 years or so.

Thomas Malthus, an 18th century economist and philosopher, said the human population increases geometrically, while food production increases arithmetically. Under this paradigm, humans would eventually be unable to produce enough food to sustain themselves.

As the human race needs more and more of the necessities of life—food, clothing and shelter being the most important—people will demand more and more from our planet. The burning questions are, as we continue to exhaust nature's bounties, as we continue to take more and more from the land, where will these necessities come from, and where will the people find land to live on?

To be sure, nature and humanity itself play a role in population numbers. As our knowledge of science and technology increases, we have been largely successful in finding more and more ways to meet the demands of the world's population. But nature requires payback in the form of raging forest fires, flooding, famine, excessive heat and cold, pandemics, and on and on. Add to these calamities the man-made number of wars that are constantly being waged somewhere around the world at any given time.

These natural and man-made disasters exact a heavy toll on the population, and yet the human numbers continue to grow at an incredible rate. Whether that rate is, in Malthus' view, ultimately unsustainable remains an open question—but it's one that can't be avoided. This can can't be kicked down the road; there is a point of diminishing returns, and then a point of no return.

There was a great book written many years ago called "The Best and the Brightest." The title should serve us well today as a message of how to deal with this existential population timebomb. We must draw from those eight billion the most skilled, accomplished, intelligent, and quick thinking people available to come to grips with a rapidly growing population and its threat to humanity's survival.

If there is a solution, this is where we will find it.

Eight billion people. Different colors, races, ethnicity. sexes, sexual preferences, religions, moral beliefs, values, shapes, sizes, etc. Some are handicapped, many are left-handed.

Each one of us is different from someone else. We may share some things in common, but not others.

And in the grand scheme of things, these differences don't matter.

But sadly and regrettably, differences do matter to those who believe they must matter. This is called bias, prejudice, self-proclaimed superiority—whatever label one wishes to attach to attitudes and behaviors that at bottom, accomplish nothing. Wars have been fought over these differences; to what end?

If an African-American man injured in an automobile accident and whose life now depends on a skilled surgeon who happens to be female Asian, none of the differences I set out previously should matter one whit.

But we all know that, for too many, they do.

With all of these differences, however, there is only one that is absolute: we are all part of the human family. There is, after all, only one humanity.

From this one humanity, there are really only two things that matter: what's in the head and what's in the heart.

The head carries the brain; the ability to read and write, gain knowledge, think analytically and critically, learn skills, apply knowledge, etc.

In the heart lies emotion, compassion, caring, love, a desire to help a fellow human, etc.

If what's in a person's head and heart meets these indicia, his or her color, race, ethnic background, sex, religion, etc., doesn't--and shouldn't--matter at all.

In the example I set out above, the only thing that matters is the surgeon's knowledge, skills and sense of caring for another member of the human race. Expand this example to other daily life occurrences and I hope I've made my point.

To solve the population problem, as well as others that cut across the entire spectrum of our existence, we must work as one human race in a never-ending search to find "the best and the brightest" from our broad and deep human pool. This can't be done, however, if we operate at cross-purposes.

Problems humanity created are problems that humanity alone can solve—if we would only choose to work as one.

OUT OF TOUCH WITH THE REST OF THE WORLD; IN TOUCH WITH THE REPUBLICAN PARTY.

Here's an example of how out of touch the Florida Republican Party is with the real world, but how in touch it is with Trump and his MAGA (now MAGAGA) crowd.

Florida GOP Chair Joe Gruters was at Mar-a-Lago for Trump's (2024 campaign) announcement. A state senator from Sarasota, Gruters co-chaired the former president's first Florida campaign in 2016, but most recently worked to reelect DeSantis, who is seen as likely to mount his own presidential campaign.

Gruters said in a text message that Trump: "Was the best President who has ever lived."

Gruters is certainly no student of American history. A large group of noted historians ranking Trump as tied with Franklin Pierce, two places above Andrew Johnson and John Buchanan--at the bottom. I supposed Gruters never heard of Abraham Lincoln, Franklin Roosevelt, George Washington, or the other presidents all ranked above Trump.

And, by the way, the ratings took place before Trump sicced his MAGA loyalists and conspiracy groups on the nation's capital almost two years ago, as well as his theft of government records.

It is no stretch of the imagination where Trump will rank when the next survey of historians is undertaken. Suffice it to say neither Pierce, Johnson or Buchanan committed criminal acts while president.

I can understand Gruters as party cheerleader and his need for advertising puffery, but advertising truth matters; historical truth matters.

But truth and history are not Republican Party strong points.

While many of the Trump worshippers, election deniers and conspiracy theory advocates were defeated, the message sent is eternal vigilance is the price of liberty. In many instances, the races were close. It's hard to understand how many millions of voters there are who deny facts, engage in crazy conspiracies, and see nothing wrong with Trump's behavior. The reality is, however, they are there and they persist.

As Arizona election denier Kari Lake said, in losing her race for governor: Arizonans "know BS when they see it." She's absolutely right; that's why she and her ilk lost. But there will always be the next election. This is why Democrats and level-headed Republicans must continue to educate the public that the Republican Party's right wing is far too extreme for America--not only today, but tomorrow as well.

BE CAREFUL WHAT YOU WISH FOR.

As soon as the number of Republicans elected to the House of Representatives reached the magic 218, confirming that the party will take control, its leadership reiterated its plans going forward—investigate, investigate, investigate.

House Speaker-designate Kevin McCarthy proudly declared "the era of one party rule is over." (He made no such declaration when the Republican Party controlled the White House and Congress, but politics is politics.)

He, as well as other leaders, casually mentioned "the border"--code word for immigration--as well as inflation and crime—street crimes (murder, robbery, assault, etc.)

They saved their verbal ammunition for other, more important, things by their design. Already, House lawmakers have floated January hearings on Hunter Biden's business dealings, a major congressional probe of the withdrawal from Afghanistan, and a new committee to investigate China's political and economic influence on the United States.

"There is a burning desire by Republicans to provide some type of oversight to the Biden administration," Rep. James Comer, R-Ky., his party's ranking member on the House Oversight Committee, told ABC News. "We're going to be under a lot of pressure to perform, but I think we will be up to the task."

According to ABC News, that pressure could include calls from lawmakers and conservative activists to impeach President Joe Biden and some Cabinet secretaries, rebut the findings of the House committee investigating the January 6 insurrection and revisit former President Donald Trump's false claims about the results of the 2020 election -- all ahead of another consequential presidential election season.

Cabinet officers facing this threat are the attorney general and secretary of homeland security. Then, there's the FBI director, and the House can't forget Dr. Anthony Fauci and his questioning of Donald Trump's handling of the COVID pandemic. (Personally, I can't wait to see the likes of Rep. Jim Jordan tangling with Dr. Fauci. I hope these committee hearings involving Biden, cabinet officers, the FBI, etc., are televised. They will make for great theater. In the meantime, it would be wise for the House to be careful what they wish for.)

To be clear about this, these investigations are being spurred by the extreme right wing of the Republican Party—the wing that will be taking over control of the House.

These investigations are not being driven by evidence already in hand of impeachable offenses or crimes. They are being driven by revenge, by payback.

This Republican-controlled House will drop the committee's investigations of Donald Trump despite clear evidence of both impeachable offenses and violations of the criminal law.

Trump's first impeachment was over a quid pro quo telephone call to the Ukraine president seeking dirt on Joe Biden's son in return for release of congressionally approved funds, which is a violation of the Impoundment Control Act.

Trump's second impeachment for inciting the January 6 riot at the capital constitutes five violations of federal law—inciting a rebellion, conspiracy to defraud the government, obstructing an official proceeding (certification of electoral college votes), witness tampering, and wire fraud.

Trump's theft of classified and other government records is a violation of the Theft Of Government Information law.

Then there's the Georgia election tampering investigation where Trump asked state officials to find the popular votes he needed to win that state's electoral college votes, and the New York investigation into Trumpland.

(The only investigation the House can stop is the second one; the others are under the authority of the Justice Department, which remains in the hands of the Democrats for at least the next two years, and state officials beyond the reach of the House.)

Trump's violations didn't require deep-digging for evidence; the transcript of Trump's call to Ukraine; the testimony and documented evidence offered by Republicans to the public through the televised House committee hearings investigating January 6; and the government records seen strewn about Trump's Mar-a-Lago estate is about as clear a picture as can be made that Trump violated a host of federal laws.

The new House leadership, however, would dump the House probe, and try to gaslight the others by adopting Trump's ludicrous smoke-and-mirrors explanations and justifications.

After this dump-off, the House would then proceed to search far and wide, looking everywhere and anywhere, calling everyone and anyone, that might—just might—provide a nugget or kernel that would allow the Republicans to throw dirt on Biden, some of his cabinet members, and anyone else who dared to question Trump's aberrational behavior during his presidency.

You would think the folks who cheerlead for law and order and who make every effort to corner the market on the rule of law would apply these standards to all equally. Forget that. When they pat themselves on the back and give themselves a round of applause for being on the "right side," they mean to apply these words only to Democrats and Republicans who have the audacity, the temerity to challenge their now shaky authoritarian.

The Republican leadership won't admit that impeachment is only for show; the Senate will never convict. And any House demands for the filing of criminal charges fall to the Justice Department that is under the Biden Administration.

Besides, Hunter Biden has been under investigation for two years now, and so far, nada.

Not to be outdone, several Democrats have now gone on record threatening to investigate Republicans who investigate Democrats. For Sen. Josh Hawley, there's a little matter of misuse of funds in connection with his campaign. He's just one example of how the tables can turn. Does anyone think all Republicans are lily white when it comes to the criminal law? Remember, it's not about conviction; it's about the glitz of investigations that is driving the House Republicans. That car can be driven by Democrats, too.

But here's the rub. If the House Republicans do as they promise, what is to prevent a scenario when the script is flipped? If the House impeaches Biden or anyone else based on evidence that as yet doesn't exist, or based on a flimsy foundation that doesn't pass the giggle test, the next time a Republican is in the White House and the House is in the hands of the Democrats, well, you get the message.

So, House Republicans, in your zeal to please the extreme wing of your party, be careful. Be very careful. Threats work both ways.

Be careful what you wish for.

HIGH CRIMES AND MISDEMEANORS ISN'T WHATEVER THE HOUSE OF REPRESENTATIVES SAYS IT IS.

Gerald Ford wasn't correct when he said, in addressing efforts to impeach Supreme Court Justice William O. Douglas, although that won't matter to the zealots and conspiracy crazed wackos who will soon be running the House.

There is a constitutional standard—"High Crimes and Misdemeanors"—that must be met, and a solid history of what the Founding Fathers meant when they included this phrase in the Constitution. If the evidence gathered by the House doesn't meet this historical standard, there is the judiciary in which the Supreme Court is the final authority of what the Constitution means.

Whether the Supreme Court would entertain what it could consider a matter fully assigned to the House and therefore not subject to judicial review, is another matter. What is important is that the Court is the final arbiter of the Constitution's meaning.

The specter of dueling impeachments depending on the parties in charge of the House and White House could give the Court pause to put the brakes on this type of tit-for-tat nonsense.

As for the threats to investigate Biden's family, we'll have to see how this plays out, but Biden and his team have been aware of this possibility for some time and you can bet the mortgage they are fully prepared for whatever these MAGA folks want to dish out. Indeed, Biden's team has already responded to this threat, saying the claims are "long-debunked conspiracy theories." Conspiracy theories are certainly nothing new to the current version of the Republican Party.

The House Republicans know their chances of passing their legislation is DOA in both the Senate and the White House, so they'll pass whatever they wish and, after predictable rejection, howl and rant against the extreme liberals, hoping it resonates with the 2024 voters. That their so-called message didn't this persuade the voters during the just-concluded election cycle doesn't matter; they will have their red meat to feed their loyalists and that's all that matters. The House Republicans appear to have no problem ignoring the voters' message to address key issues rather than pander to the extremists who want Biden blood in revenge for the impeachment of Donald Trump. They ignore the mass electorate at their political peril.

If the Republican Party continues to follow the path of the extremists, they can kiss the White House goodbye in 2024 and hopefully beyond. And they may just lose the House, too.

A NOTE ABOUT TAX CUTS, WELFARE PROGRAMS, CRIME AND IMMIGRATION.

Predictably, the House Republican leadership, energized by their takeover of the House of Representatives, said it's time to "get America back on track" by passing tax cuts, limiting government by "getting (it) off our backs" as Ronald Reagan would say, tackling crime and fixing the border.

That sounds so good to taxpayers. After all, who wouldn't want their taxes reduced? Who doesn't favor "getting government off our backs?" No one opposes tackling crime and dealing with immigration.

But as is the case, the devil's in the details. Let's look at tax cuts and limiting government.

The unalterable fact is every government program costs money. And every program that is now on the books was put there to address a need at the time of enactment. To be sure, some programs have come and gone, but those that remain are there because there has been a demonstrated need for them, and the government acted to address that need.

In 2022, 65 million Americans were on one or more of the nation's 83 welfare programs, costing approximately $1.5 trillion. That's more than 20% of the entire population that's on some form of welfare. Each of these programs costs money that must be raised from taxes. Every dollar that is cut from tax revenue impacts these programs in some form or another.

So, the first question to be asked is if there is going to be a tax cut, how big will those cuts be, and what programs will be reduced or perhaps eliminated? Further, each program requires administration to ensure against fraud, mismanagement of funds, etc. As second question is how many government employees will lose their jobs as a result of tax and program cuts?

(There are also non-welfare programs that are funded by tax dollars that will also have to be cut if tax revenue is to be slashed. The infrastructure legislation passed earlier this year comes to mind. Which bridges won't be repaired? Which roads will remain riddled with potholes? And on and on.)

Every person whose welfare benefit is reduced or eliminated will have to replace that lost income somehow. The typical first reaction is "well, they should get a job." Fair question, except for a couple of things. First, there has to be an employer willing to hire a welfare recipient. Second, that recipient has to be trained in some manner or form so that he/she can do the job properly. That takes some time. Third, if the welfare recipient is a single mother of infants or small children, how is she to provide for her children if she has to leave home for a job? Day care costs money, too.

I could go on and on, but while it's easy to say "get a job," once again, the devil's in the details. It is self-evident that cutting taxes has a strong ripple effect throughout our entire nation's fundamental economic and social system.

The most commonly relied upon welfare programs are: Medicaid, Supplemental Security Income (SSI), Supplemental Nutrition Assistance Program (SNAP), Child's Health Insurance Program (CHIP), Temporary Assistance to Needy Families. housing assistance, .Earned Income Tax Credit (EITC). These, along with Social Security, make up around 80% of the nation's annual budget.

According to census data, the following is a snapshot that shows how much of the population depends on these social services programs:

- 13.7% of the total population received SNAP in 2015.
- Among those receiving energy aid, 13.5% also received SSI and 20.6% were between the ages of 50 and 64 in 2019.
- 34.7% of households included someone who was receiving Social Security benefits in 2018.
- 69.6% of households where someone was receiving free or reduced-price school meals also included someone who was receiving Medicaid/CHIP in 2013.
- Among individuals receiving benefits from Medicaid/ CHIP *and* WIC, 58.5% were also getting SNAP in 2016.

- 50.1% of those receiving SNAP, TANF, *and* rental subsidies were Black and 27.7% were Hispanic in 2014.
- 58.7% of households receiving both Social Security *and* energy aid included just one person living alone in 2017.

The fact is we have a lot of Americans on welfare that's costing taxpayers a lot of money.

Now for crime and immigration.

Another fact is that poverty and crime go hand in hand. As the poverty level increases, so does street crime. No surprise here.

The House Republican plan to address crime is to put another 100,000 officers on the streets. This, of course, costs money. They haven't yet explained how they're going to pay for this while reducing taxes.

There's really only one way—cut welfare programs even further. This will inevitably lead to more poverty and its major consequence, more crime. More crime means more police on the street—which means more government expenditures. Which leads to further cuts in welfare programs, and on and on. The ripple, or domino, effect should be obvious.

Pointedly, in their stump speeches about crime, there's no talk about jobs programs, intervention programs—which also costs money--or reducing the number of firearms on the streets.

Tackling the border crisis will also cost money for more border agents, more employees to deal with the influx of asylum seekers, and everything else associated with managing the nation's immigration system. Again, if tax revenue is depleted, how will the Republicans deal with these additional immigration manpower costs?

These are just some of the questions yet to be answered by the newly energized House leaders.

Meanwhile, we await the House Republicans' plan to cut taxes, reduce expenditures, and cut welfare and other government programs, while solving our crime and immigration problems which will inevitably cost more money. We will see how they address this vicious cycle.

The difference now is that they can't rely on slogans; they have to provide a concrete, workable plan of action. Talk is cheap. Now they have to show they can govern while they're spending large sums of money on investigations into all things Biden.

IF THE RUSSIANS CROSSING THE UKRAINE BORDER IS AN INVASION, WHY ISN'T THE MASS OF HUMANITY CROSSING AMERICA'S SOUTHERN BORDER ALSO CALLED AN INVASION? MY ANSWER.

I suppose because the Russians attacked Ukraine in an act of war, while the other involves people from Latin American countries seeking a better life, possibly reminded of what it says on the Statue of Liberty: "Give me your tired, your poor, your huddled masses yearning to breathe free." In the late 1800s, conditions primarily in Europe, such as crop failure, land and job shortages, rising taxes, and famine, caused many to come here because America was perceived as the land of economic opportunity.

Other factors included employment opportunities in a growing nation, the need to escape a violent conflict, environmental factors, educational pursuits, or to reunite with family. Except for the American Indian, just about everyone here now are descendants of immigrants. There is, of course, a point of oversaturation, but this can be dealt with through a commonsense immigration program.... something we don't have now.

Those who believe a wall or fence along the Mexican border will cure the problem overlook a vital fact: the degree of difficulty it is to secure our nation's borders. Those borders include not only along Mexico but Canada and the east and west coasts as well. We have a long border that can be crossed by both land, sea and air. In fact, the initial immigrants--the Puritans and Pilgrims--came here via the sea. The Mexican coastline is about 2,000 miles long; the Canadian coastline is about 5,500 miles long. The Atlantic coastline is about 2,165 miles long; the Pacific coastline is about 1,300 miles long. That's about 11,000 miles of coast to protect.

If the focus is only on the south, it's worth noting that our nation was attacked on 9/11 via the air flying over the Canadian and Atlantic coast borders. If attackers can reach us by air, what is to prevent immigrants from using more points of entry than the Mexican border? While it is true that the vast majority of immigrants are coming from the southern border, people who are desperate enough to want to flee their homeland will find a way through the most porous of borders--south, as well and north, east and west. For example, if they can't come through the Mexican border, there's always the coastline of Louisiana, Alabama and, largest of all, Florida. I don't think we can build walls or post fences across the Gulf of Mexico. It doesn't take much to note that people who want something bad enough will find the weakest link to attack. If it's not the Mexican border; it will be another one. This is human nature. It will take policies, not walls or fences alone, to manage the flow of immigrants.

IMMORTALITY: PLANT A TREE, HAVE A CHILD, WRITE A BOOK

Many years ago, as a young man, the father of a friend of mine told me something that has stuck with me over the years, and still resonates today. He said every man should do three things in his life: plant a tree, have a child, and write a book.

As I mulled this over in my mind, I thought how relatively simple it seemed to accomplish all three, but then I move on and didn't give it much more thought until I reached adulthood.

One day, after I married and was awaiting the birth of my first child, I recalled what I was told years earlier, so I decided to find the source of his words of wisdom. It turns out that's exactly what they were: words of wisdom.

The quote is: "Every man (or more correctly, person) should plant a tree, have a child, and write a book.." It is attributed to the Talmud (the primary source of Jewish religious law and Jewish theology) and Jose Martí, Cuban revolutionary and poet. Other authors have waxed on it, most notably Ernest Hemingway.

Why these three things? These all live on after us, ensuring a measure of immortality.

Life is short. Each of us gets one shot at it. There are no do-overs, no replays (instant or otherwise) and no second chances to start over. There is no guarantee at birth that each of us will live from childhood to adulthood to old age. It is well to do the best we can, the most we can, while we can.

Planting a tree means giving back to the Earth whatever each person has taken from it. A tree will also survive generations and seed itself, allowing for growth of generations of more trees. If the tree is taken for wood, that product will be used to build a house or some other item that will last longer than the life of the person who planted that tree. In this way, immortality of the planter is assured.

You may be familiar with "plant a tree" programs. The Nature Conservancy's Plant a Billion Trees campaign is a major forest restoration program. Our goal is to plant a billion trees across the planet to slow the connected crises of climate change and biodiversity loss.

If you haven't planted your tree yet, or want to plant more, this is one of many programs that serve this purpose. There are others that can be found simply by checking the various websites.

Having and raising a child provides the knowledge that even after we are gone our legacy lives on through our offspring. Depression and war prevented my father from living his dream. He wanted his children--my late brother and me--to live the kind of life denied to him. Although his struggles and frustrations were many, his expectations for us were high. It didn't matter what we wanted to be; he just wanted us to excel at it. He instilled in us a strong value system, compelling us to behave in a certain manner: study hard, work hard, have gratitude and compassion, marry sensibly, have a home and children. In essence, what he wanted was for his children to fulfill his own unfinished dreams through them.

I have a feeling that this story isn't an isolated one.

The third path to immortality is writing a book. This shows unique intelligence, knowledge and literacy necessary to prepare a lengthy written composition. It is your own work, perhaps influenced by others, but set out in your own personal style.

I would include other written forms that have the same permanent effect as a book. For example, songs, poetry, plays and articles. Many of our greatest songwriters, poets and playwrights never wrote a book, yet their works stand the test of time. Articles reflecting the author's expertise or interest also serve as a permanent written exemplar of one's intelligence, knowledge, experience, etc. I wrote hundreds of byline articles as a newspaper reporter and editor, and dozens of law-related articles in my career, but never wrote a book.

That is, until 2012 when I wrote my first one while recovering from major orthopedic surgery. It was a memoir for my family, especially my children and grandchildren. This was followed by two novellas and a second memoir. Two years ago, I started writing extensively on social media. I retained each Facebook post and have written three books that consist of those posts, and I'm currently working on the fourth that will, of course, include this post.

A reputable publishing company ensures that each book is: provided its copyright date, deposited in the Library of Congress with an assigned number, and made available to such book sellers as Barnes and Noble and Amazon, as well as the publishing company itself.

There you have it. No need to search for the magic elixir of life, or visit St. Augustine and drink from the Fountain of Youth (I have. Several times. It doesn't work.). The path to immortality is in three parts. If you haven't yet planted a tree, do so. It's easy, especially if you have a backyard.

If you haven't written that book, published a song. poem, play or article, get going on it. Each of us has led a unique life. What not tell your story? Once you draft an outline in chronological form, you will be surprised how easy the words will flow. Trust me on this, I know because I did precisely that.

I'll leave the childbearing part to you.

"IT WAS A TIME WHEN STRANGERS WERE WELCOME HERE."

This is a line from a song entitled "The Immigrant" written by that great singer/songwriter Neil Sedaka. The song mentions harbors opening their doors to the young searching foreigner coming to live in the light of liberty. The lyrics describe boats carrying dreamers of a brighter future arriving at our shores. He says:

It was time when strangers were welcome here.
Music would play they tell me the days were sweet and clear.
It was a sweeter tune and there was so much room
That people could come from everywhere.

Then, he digresses to describe what appears most relevant today:

Now he arrives with hopes and his heart set on miracles
Come to marry his fortune with a hand full of promises
To find they've closed the door, they don't want him anymore
There isn't any more to go around.
Turning away he remembers he once heard a legend
That spoke of a mystical magical land called America.

This song was written in 1975!

This "magical land" once prided itself on being a melting pot; a society where many types of people from all over the world blended together as one. People of different races, religions, ethnicity, culture came together despite these differences to coexist, assimilate and live together as one nation. Through economic hardship and war, America's diversity proved again and again that we could overcome any burden because we were one nation dedicated to form "a more perfect union," and indivisible, and with the aspiration of living "with liberty and justice for all."

Between 1850 and 1920, during a period called the Age of Mass Migration, more than 30 million Europeans immigrated to the United States, and the share of foreign born in the United States' population was even higher than today. Such massive migration, however, was interrupted by two major shocks – World War I and the Immigration Acts (1921 and 1924) – that resulted in a large variation not only in the number but also in the composition of immigrants moving to America during this period.

In the last five decades, the number of foreign-born individuals living in the United States has increased more than five-fold, jumping from nine million in 1970 to 50 million in 2017. Not surprisingly, this trend has sparked a heated political debate. Proposals to introduce or tighten immigration restrictions are becoming increasingly common, and support for populist, right-wing public officials pushing what is branded as an anti-immigration agenda has been rising steadily.

Two main reasons seem to be driving anti-immigrant sentiment. The first is economic in nature: the negative effect of immigration on employment and wages for Americans already here (natives). This may well be the key factor behind the political discontent here. Although this argument is compelling, and supported by some studies, evidence suggests that immigrants have a negligible, or even positive, impact on natives' earnings, in part by globally addressing the job market and increasing the minimum wage.

The second reason is the backlash triggered by cultural differences between immigrants and natives. Both today and in the past, politicians highlight the possibility that immigrants' cultural diversity might represent an obstacle to social cohesion and a menace to the values of already existing communities. This didn't seem to be an overarching problem 100 or so years ago, but it is today.

There is a third factor—one touted recently: crime. However, studies show that the population and influx of immigrants over the years has not influenced the crime rate.

As of 2017, according to Gallup polls, almost half of Americans agreed that immigrants make crime worse. But is it true that immigration drives crime? Many studies have shown that it doesn't.

Immigrant populations in the United States have been growing fast for decades now. Crime during the same period, however, has moved in the opposite direction, with the national rate of violent crime today well below what it was in 1980.

According to data from the Marshall Project, a large majority of the areas have many more immigrants today than they did in 1980 and fewer violent crimes. The Marshall Project extended the study's data up to 2016, showing that crime fell more often than it rose even as immigrant populations grew almost across the board.

"In 136 metro areas, almost 70 percent of those studied, the immigrant population increased between 1980 and 2016 while crime stayed stable or fell. The number of areas where crime and immigration both increased was much lower — 54 areas, slightly more than a quarter of the total. The 10 places with the largest increases in immigrants all had lower levels of crime in 2016 than in 1980.

And yet the argument that immigrants bring crime to America drove many of the policies enacted or proposed by the Trump Administration: restrictions to entry, travel and visas; heightened border enforcement; a wall along the border with Mexico. This, despite the fact that while the immigrant population in the country has more than doubled since 1980, overall violent crime has decreased by more than 50 percent.

For example, a Texas study found that undocumented immigrants had substantially lower crime rates than native-born citizens and legal immigrants across a range of felony offenses. Relative to undocumented immigrants, American-born citizens are over two times more likely to be arrested for violent crimes, 2.5 times more likely to be arrested for drug crimes, and over four times more likely to be arrested for property crimes.

Yet, for many, perception is reality, and perceptions die hard. Facts and statistics are of no importance to someone who buys into perceptions or who's been a victim of crime or knows someone who's been victimized. If a single reported crime involves someone here illegally, that image is projected to the point that people believe there is a crime wave attributable to illegal aliens.

There is no need to recite the history of inventions and innovations produced by immigrants that made the quality of life in America unsurpassed anywhere else in the world. There have been plenty of books written on that subject.

But now there is a prevalent attitude that we've allowed enough immigrants into America, and our nation's population is growing to such an extent that there won't be enough resources to feed, clothe and shelter a growing population further burdened by a growing influx of immigrants. Hence, we have governors who, instead of protecting the physical well-being of those who wind up in their states, put them on airplanes at taxpayers' expense and send them to other states that are more concerned about their health and well-being. I trust this is not an example of what these public officials mean by compassionate conservatism.

These matters concerning population expansion and limited resources are certainly legitimate questions that will have to be addressed, not only in America, but throughout the world as the population explosion continues to rage.

But walls, fences, etc., are not a solution; they won't keep out people "yearning to be free," echoing the words that appear on the Statue of Liberty. A comprehensive immigration plan that provides for eventual full citizenship and includes mobility relocation, employment, housing, education, and possible application of those relevant programs, services and opportunities currently available to natives but structured for immigrants seems a sensible way to go.

We are all the ancestors of immigrants. Think what would have happened if the doors were shut permanently on past generations like many are trying to do now. Or our grandparents and their parents were put on airplanes and sent who knows where.

I wouldn't be writing this, and you wouldn't be reading this.

SHOULD THE TRUMP SPECIAL PROSECUTOR CONSIDER FILING ALL CHARGES FOR A SINGLE TRIAL, OR DIVIDE THE CHARGES FOR A SECOND TRIAL?

A question has been raised about the special prosecutor appointed to investigate former president Donald Trump for possible crimes committed on the January 6 attack on the nation's capital, and his removal of government records from the White House to his Mar-a-Lago estate.

Specifically, the question concerns whether the prosecutor should bring fewer charges in one prosecution, saving the others for future prosecutions, or bring all charges at one time. The reason for this question is out of concern over confusing a jury when so much evidence has to be considered in light of a multiplicity of charges.

There are several reasons for bringing all charges at one time.

First, prosecutors want to avoid the risk of a double jeopardy claim. The law of double jeopardy has its complexities and failure to charge a specific crime can be subsumed into one for which a defendant is found not guilty.

Second, the statute of limitations might run out on a crime not charged, thereby forever barring a prosecution. There may be other practical reasons for bringing all possible charges at one time even at the risk of confusing a jury. (The risk here is usually when one or two jurors become confused; it's rare for an entire panel to become confused. In this circumstance, a prosecutor puts his faith in the hands of those jurors who "get it" to explain to the others, with the hope of bringing them around.)

Third, the law generally favors bringing all charges at one time. This takes into consideration the time and expenditure of judicial resources necessary for one trial as opposed to two or more; more time expended for the judges, the prosecutors, jurors, witnesses, courthouse facilities, etc. There may well be circumstances where more than one trial against a single defendant may be necessary, but those reasons would have to be clearly spelled out and be of a profound nature to overcome the favored single trial involving all crimes.

Fourth, a jury considering multiple crimes may be more inclined to find a defendant guilty of one or more if they are given a wider choice, believing that the prosecution wouldn't have filed so many charges if it didn't have enough evidence to justify a conviction on at least some crimes. If the choice is up or down on a single charge, or even two charges, a jury might be more inclined to acquit both.

Fifth, there's the possibility of loss of evidence. As time goes by, witnesses become incompetent due to age, or die; documents become misplaced or lost. The best time to prosecute is earlier, rather than later.

I think when the special counsel in the Trump investigations makes his determination, he will go for the jugular on all possible crimes.

There are several reasons for this, I believe. First, these are not detailed, fact-intense tax or corporate finance or management crimes that require voluminous paperwork and long, drawn-out testimony from fiscal experts.

Second, the potential crimes against Trump have been well publicized, thereby reducing the need to educate a jury in great detail.

Third, the potential crimes are not complex or convoluted; what happened on January 6 is relatively straightforward, judging from the live testimony before the House committee investigating January 6. The same is true regarding the removal of government records to his private estate. While the defenses are unique because the potential charges against a former president who acted while president are unprecedented, those defenses don't affect the evidence itself of criminal acts.

IS MASS SHOOTING THE PRICE OF FREEDOM IN AMERICA? PERHAPS IT'S TIME FOR A FORM OF STRICT LIABILITY.

The headline screams a tragedy we've seen too many times before. The latest says

"Gunman kills 5 at LGBTQ nightclub in Colorado Springs."

This is not the first time patrons of a nightclub were victims of a mass shooter. Over the years, mass murder victims were in African-American churches, Jewish Synagogues, malls, schools, shopping centers, movie theaters, hospitals, motels, hotels, parade routes, restaurants, supermarkets, just about every place where people congregate. There is no such place off limits to a mass shooter and mass murder.

Each time we learn of a mass shooting, each time we see reports of the horror, the loss, the anguish, the pain and suffering, we hear the same old refrain: thoughts and prayers for the victims, outrage over this "senseless act;" then virtual silence or a shrug of the shoulders...until the next time, when we hear these same words again.

And make no mistake about it, there will be a next time. And the sad reality is anyone of us could be there when it happens.

The perpetrator is portrayed as mentally ill, angry over his treatment by others, ridiculed on social media, taking out a grudge against others; the profiles are fairly predictable.

The act of mass shooter is "senseless" to the rational-minded, common sensical, compassionate person. The perpetrator is never a reasonable, well-adjusted, caring person. These descriptions are more designed to give the public some comfort that these horrific acts defy good judgment and represent isolated, albeit deviant, behavior by a very few. This, however, is of little comfort to the victims, and doesn't give the public a warm, fuzzy feeling about visiting these places of public accommodation.

It has become useless to ask—indeed beg---for a ban on assault weapons or the passage of universal background checks. The reality of today's political climate make these non-starters.

The message that is sent from the gun advocates is that these mass shootings is the price of freedom in America. They believe the Second Amendment is absolute and any effort to address this epidemic of violent acts—regardless of whether they're hate crimes or just some crazed or troubled person acting in revenge—must not infringe on anyone's individual unfettered right to carry a weapon of his/her choice, either concealed or openly, for self-protection, or for any purpose he/she wishes without question.

Sadly, these mass shootings are just a part of violent crime besetting our communities. Here in Tallahassee, a group of civic leaders and law enforcement personnel have been scratching their heads trying to come up with a plan to tackle an uptick of street crime.

This group, a task force, came up with a 15-point list of action items that include scheduling citywide prayer services; supporting funding for crime prevention programs; developing military boot camp targeting at-risk youth; developing Police Athletic Clubs; expanding programs directed toward employment for at-risk youth; developing ordinances to prevent and prohibit violence; working to provide jobs, affordable housing, job training and mentoring programs; supporting after-school programs; and essentially have more communitywide meetings, devote more resources, spend more money, and bring the community together.

Something is noticeably missing from this list as reported in the local newspaper. Not a single word mentions guns or firearms. There is nothing about how easy it is to get one's hands on these weapons, or what can be done in today's political environment to address this.

The seminal question is how do you keep guns out of the hands of those who are desirous of using them to commit crimes?

Too many pleas for substantive action on guns have fallen on deaf ears.

But there is one possible approach that hasn't been given much attention, yet would have some appeal especially to those who are Second Amendment absolutists.

It's called strict liability.

Lawyers are most familiar with what this means. Essentially, strict liability in criminal and civil law is a standard of liability under which a person is legally responsible for the consequences flowing from an activity even in the absence of fault or criminal intent on the part of the defendant.

Those who champion individual accountability and personal responsibility should support a form of strict liability for holding accountable someone whose conduct had a causal connection to the commission of a violent crime involving a firearm.

Local law enforcement is constantly reminding citizens to lock their cars and not leave their valuables in their vehicles. Among the valuables listed are firearms. This serves as adequate notice of what personal responsibility looks like, particularly with regard to firearms.

For example, if a car owner leaves his/her gun on the car seat, and someone breaks into the vehicle, steals the weapon and uses it in a crime, why shouldn't the car owner be held accountable for his own conduct which led to the ultimate crime? As a presumably responsible and knowledgeable gun owner, he/she should be held to assure that the weapon doesn't fall into the wrong hands. He shouldn't be held harmless and free of any liability for leaving his weapon where someone with bad intentions might easily access it.

Another example is if a perpetrator is a juvenile living with one or more parents who own a firearm, why shouldn't the parents—or legal guardian in those circumstances—be held accountable for failing to make sure that their juvenile can't get his/her hands on that weapon? Similarly, a parent or guardian shouldn't be held harmless and free of liability for leaving his firearm lying around the house or apartment in a manner easily accessible by that juvenile.

This strict liability could also apply to any adult living with a parent who leaves his/her weapon in such a place that a child of adult years could gain easy access and commit a horrific crime.

The most notable point about strict liability is that nothing about it implicates in any way a person's right under the Second Amendment to purchase, own or carry a firearm.

I understand the devil's in the details regarding such legislation. If, for example, a gun owner locks the weapon in a safe and that safe is broken into, the owner should be presumed to have done everything reasonably possible to prevent access to that weapon. There may well be other examples of a gun owner acting reasonably under the particular circumstances that wouldn't justify applying strict liability. But this is what we have legislatures and local governments for.

The simple fact is there are ways to structure a strict liability law that protects the gun owner who acted sensibly and reasonably in assuring that there is no easy access to that weapon, while targeting those who leave their weapon(s) where they can be easily obtained.

Strict liability would send a strong message to parents, guardians, vehicle owners—and others similarly situated— that buying and owning a firearm comes with profound responsibilities. The seminal point is a simple one: the exercise of a constitutional right where deadly weapons are involved must come with at least some cognizable and meaningful level of personal responsibility and accountability to assure that the firearm doesn't fall into the wrong hands.

People's lives depend on it. Your life may depend on it.

DEALING WITH HATE: UNIVERSAL CONDEMNATION AND OSTRACIZATION, AND UNIVERSAL COMPASSION.

The latest mass shooting--this one at a gay nightclub in Colorado Springs--once again demonstrates the level of hate that has engulfed our nation over the past few years.

Driven at least in part by a sense of self-supremacy, victims have been African-Americans, Jews, Hispanics, Arabs, Asians, LGTBQ—just about any group or individual that is different.

The America that was once a great melting pot of diverse cultures and backgrounds is now a source of fear among many in the majority as they sense a loss of what America once was. The bottom line here is the Caucasian population is declining as the population of minorities is increasing, and this coupled with heated rhetoric, is fanning the flames.

This reality, growing over time, created a tension that was tapped into by some of our political leaders who saw the seething anger lying just below the surface. They exploited this situation by their rhetoric that, like a pressure cooker, led to an explosion manifested by hateful speech and violence.

Sadly, we now have laws that deal with hate speech and hate crimes.

Recently, we witnessed individual minority group members level their hate against other minorities.

Rapper Kanye West directed a diatribe against Jews, using just about every bigoted false and baseless perception and stereotype to make his point.

You would think that a Black man, familiar with his race being victimized and vilified by bigoted hate speech and worse, and stung by false and baseless perceptions and stereotypes, would be sympathetic to other minority individuals and groups. But that's not the case here.

If the shoe were on the other foot, and he was the victim of hateful speech, vile slurs, and similarly stung, he and his supporters would raise holy hell against those vicious hatemongers. It's horrible when victimized, It must never be acceptable to victimize others.

We can sadly recall stories of minorities being beaten and killed solely because they are different from the haters. Blacks gunned down in their churches; Jews assaulted in their synagogues; Asians, Arabs, Hispanics assaulted and beaten on the streets solely because they're different; LGTBQs killed and injured in nightclubs again only because they're different.

After the thoughts and prayers, and the funerals and recoveries, we go back to doing our business, until the next cycle begins.

The level of hate can't be sustained. Hate is a cancer that will destroy unless it's excised from the body.

There are ways to deal with hate and its tragic consequences. The first step is universal condemnation and ostracization of the perpetrator. No excuses and no forgiveness without legitimate remorse or contrition, and only after serving the penalty for the conduct.

Our government leaders, instead of stoking violence as some have over the past few years, must speak as one in condemning in the most vigorous manner possible, this vile and egregious behavior.

Ostracization and isolation of the haters is a necessity. They must never be given any reason to believe they represent a larger group that supports such deviant behavior. They must be made to feel that their thoughts and actions are alien to what America stands for. They must also be ostracized by family, friends and associates as well. In sum, all fingers must point directly to the haters.

They must be made to know that they will carry such behavior with them for the rest of their lives. Their schooling, employment—indeed, all of the benefits of living in a free society---will be implicated by their hateful behavior, even if their conduct consists only of the kind we recall in Charlottesville, Virginia in 2017 when groups of white supremacists marched against the Jews.

We saw much of this same hatred on display on January 6 in Washington, D.C.

The third prong is universal compassion for the victims. Let the haters—and the rest of the world---know that these innocent individuals and groups have the full support and caring of a grateful nation. This will require a single voice from our elected and appointed leaders. Sadly, some of those leaders continue to be part of the problem.

If they can't—or won't—convince their followers that hate of this kind has no place in our country, and treat the victims of hate with a strong showing of compassion, then we need to seek out our better angels and replace these charlatans. They are frauds and dividers; not real leaders in bringing people together.

No more thoughts and prayers. No more shrugging of the shoulders. No more waiting for something to happen to heal the wounds of hate. Cast the haters from our midst.

Enough is enough.

"LIVE AND LET LIVE" OR "MIND YOUR OWN BUSINESS."

In my most recent posts, I discussed two pressing problems besetting our country: guns and hate. Realizing that it's easier to complain than it is to offer a solution, I proposed strict liability for a parent or guardian of a shooter, and the universality of condemnation and isolation for the hater and universality of compassion for the victim. The purpose behind this is to drive the hater back from whence he came.

There is yet another problem that has grown with great intensity over the past few years. To put it directly, we have too many people telling others how to live their lives.

We used to pride ourselves for living in a nation where majority rules, but with respect for the minority; sadly, that's not the case anymore; now, it depends on the issue. A vocal minority with deep pockets will too often control the dialogue and compel government to bend to their will, despite the will of the majority—even if that majority is substantial.

We also prided ourselves on preserving and protecting the most fundamental aspect of a democracy, free and fair elections. Sadly, this isn't the case anymore, at least in some parts of the country.

Now, it's become acceptable and even mainstream to challenge election results by a losing candidate, even when there isn't a scintilla of evidence supporting the election denier. That about 50 million people bought into election denial even after the courts found no supportive evidence is dangerous for the well-being of our nation. Several candidates in the recent election cycle also took the election denial route, as if it's now the thing to do to explain a loss. This nonsense must not be allowed to become fashionable.

Both the scoffing of majority will and denying the fairness of an election seriously undermine democratic principles. Those who clamor for getting back to basics would do well to follow their own advice and get back to the basics of respecting majority rule and honoring election results.

The phrase "live and let live" is ancient and comes from the Dutch. It simply means each person should let other people behave in the way that they want to, and not criticize them for behaving differently from you. In a more direct manner, it means "mind your own business;" stay out of those matters that don't affect you, and don't force others to live their lives in order to satisfy how you choose to live yours.

A profound example of this is the perplexing and bedeviling issue of abortion. If a person doesn't believe in abortion, that's fine, then don't have one. But if a person believes in abortion, don't tell that person she must conform to your view. That person should have the same right to have an abortion as one who chooses not to.

There is no doubt that a significant majority of Americans favor abortion with varying limitations and conditions. What they don't agree with is a flat ban on abortion preferred by a vocal minority.

There are ways to accommodate both views by banning it in local communities where a majority of voters don't want it, and allowing it with restrictions in communities where a majority of voters approve it. This mustn't be done on a state-by-state basis; since in the words of the late House Speaker Tip O'Neill," all politics is local," this decision should be left to local communities. This approach doesn't unduly burden a woman, unlike a state-by-state approach where a legislature can ban abortions for the entire state, thereby placing an inordinate burden on a woman who has to travel to another state for the procedure. An example here is if the voters in city A vote to ban abortion, but city B voters approve of the procedure however limited or restricted (presumably along the line of Roe v. Wade or any further developmental standard), the votes in both cities should be honored.

Another example is school curriculum. If a parent wants his/her child to learn about the harsh lessons of history, including matters of race, etc., that parent should have that choice. If, however, a parent wants his/her child to avoid being exposed to that history because it may hurt feelings or cause psychological discomfort, that parent should similarly have that choice. (Of course, under the latter choice, the result will be ignorance instead of knowledge.) If this requires curriculum adjustment to accommodate both interests, school administrators and teachers are well able to make provisions for both versions to be taught.

One way to accomplish this is to identify a block of time when these more sensitive matters are taught, inform the parents of this, and have them choose. If a parent doesn't want the child to attend classes during that specific teaching, alternative provisions can be made for that child. It doesn't take rocket science to figure out how to accommodate both sides.

If college students believe a certain viewpoint is being favored over another, simply have the appropriate campus organization invite speakers with contrasting viewpoints. If, for example, the campus Young Democrats invite a speaker, there should be nothing prohibiting the Young Republicans from inviting a speaker of their choice. If the selected speaker in highly controversial, or even incendiary, there are rules in place to deal with all eventualities while being faithful to freedom of speech. The bottom line here is that different viewpoints make a college and university a place where ideas and views can be freely exchanged. Allowing organizations to invite speakers goes to the very heart of a democracy.

If a speaker with a particular viewpoint is invited by the university or college, than the institution is obligated to at least do due diligence to invite speakers with different viewpoints. It isn't difficult for university officials to inquire of clubs or organizations of possible speakers for invitation.

To be sure, there are other examples of intrusions and forced choices. For all of these, practice "live and let live."

The point of this brief narrative, however, is as old as the hills, but has a new catchphrase: stay in your own lane.

"WHAT CAN PROFESSORS EXPECT FROM THEIR STUDENTS? APPARENTLY NOT MUCH."

This is the headline over an article that appears in today's Tallahassee Democrat.

It strikes at the heart of an issue that should send shock waves through our country: are university and college curricula being systematically dumbed down, cleansed of difficult but critically important elements, to keep students happy?

There are studies that answer YES to this question, further noting that colleges have dumbed down their academic standards to keep students from dropping out of school. Evidently, higher education institutions can't afford to lose tuition, book and related revenues by dropouts, and communities can't afford to lose consumers who keep businesses afloat around campuses. Students pay rent, buy food, etc. Student economic impact is not lost on these institutions. So, rather than raising the bridge, they lower the river.

Several additional questions are also raised by this writer:

Who are the students to question the contents of a course's curriculum? I thought academic studies were purposed to educate and prepare students to enter a demanding and competitive workforce. In every business, professional and vocational discipline, we want and expect the best and the brightest. Would you want a physician who graduated from a university that provided only "easier" courses to perform delicate orthopedic or heart surgery on you? The answer is self-evident.

Are grades going up because the course material has been dumbed down? If a college or university prides itself on high grades and high graduation rates, are those numbers the result of easing the students' workload?

There is serious discussion about doing away with tests such as the state bar exams as well as other professional exams designed to test overall knowledge and comprehension. If the goal is to make college life easier, this is one way to do it, but the consequences of a less-educated generation are damning. As other countries increase their education standards, our nation can't afford to go in the opposite direction.

Firing a professor because some students complain the course is too difficult raises the obvious question of who's in charge of American education, the educators or the students?

Our nation depends on a well-educated citizenry. If the quality of the product is reduced or diminished, it should be obvious who will suffer.

THE SAD STATE OF MASS SHOOTINGS IN AMERICA.

Just go on any search engine, type in "mass shootings," and you'll find a lengthy--and growing--list. One report shows more than 600 mass shootings this year alone. After the Walmart shooting, we heard the typical responses: "senseless act," "thoughts and players are with the victims," "my heart goes out to the victims," etc. We've heard it all before. And nothing will happen until the next one, followed again by the same wailing that is full of sound and fury, but signifies nothing.

It has reached a point where several foreign countries have issued travel warnings of varying degrees about violence.

There are two things in common with every mass shooting: a man and a firearm. Since 1982, only three mass shootings were committed by a woman. In every instance, however, a firearm was the instrument of death and injury.

Too many seeking more to deflect than to deal with the problem, cite mental health as the cause. But a perpetrator may be legally competent and show no physical evidence of his intended crime. And we know that all-too-often telling signs are missed or ignored for fear of making a mistake or of getting involved in other people's business--with tragic consequences.

In a recent article by Julian Zeliger, he discusses a possible connection that at least in part explains how we got here. Zeliger, author of "The Presidency of Donald Trump: A First Historical Perspective," traces a direct line from Newt Gingrich's Tea Party to Sarah Palin's rugged Americanism to Donald Trump. Gingrich attacked "liberal elitists" and welfare giveaways. Palin was a former Alaska mayor and was serving as Alaska's governor when she was chosen as Republican Party vice presidential nominee by John McCain in 2008. Her good looks and straight talk were appealing, until she proved to be an embarrassment to the party's rank-and-file.

She was seriously uninformed on crucial issues; claimed she could see Russia from Alaska; and couldn't name a single newspaper or magazine she read regularly. To make matters worse during the campaign, she repeatedly said things that weren't true or things published on the Internet. Although Palin lost her bid for Congress, Zeliger says she paved the way for Trump and Trumpism.

Gingrich gave us anger; an "I'm mad as hell, and I'm not going to take it anymore" mentality. Palin, the gun-toting rugged individualist from the wilds of the last frontier, mixed anger with ignorance, and made this fashionable. Trump took the anger, ignorance and lying to unprecedented heights, and the rest is history. There are steps that can be taken, however, to deal with this spike in gun violence and mass shootings. They just require courage and common sense.

Purchasing a firearm should be more difficult than buying a car or a home, or a loaf of bread for that matter. A prospective purchaser should show evidence of passing a state-certified course on use, management and care of a firearm. He should also provide evidence from a state-licensed physician attesting to mental and emotional fitness to own a weapon. Universal background checks and elimination of loopholes should be a given. If demonstrating competence and fitness is too much of a burden, ownership and use should be denied.

For Second Amendment absolutists, remember this: the words of that amendment are the same today as they were 50 years ago when weapons of war and law enforcement were used only by those involved in one or the other. What has changed is the interpretation of those words as societal stressors increased.

Two-income families. Cost of living increases; wage stagnation. Increased stress on mental health and overall well-being. And easier access to handguns and weapons of war. The re-interpretation of those words is part of the problem and does nothing to address a cure. One thing is absolutely certain: doing nothing is unacceptable. Too many are being killed and maimed while our so-called leaders shrug their shoulders and raise their hands in a "what can we do" gesture.

There is one certain thing that some of these politicos can do: they can cut the divisive, bigoted, antisemitic rhetoric and stop giving aid and comfort to hatred. Instead of socializing with known bigots and haters, they should be calling them out for being the low-life that they are.

And those who socialize with these bigots and make hatred acceptable should be called out for what they are. If these folks can't--or won't--address the hatred that breeds these mass murderers, and deal with mass murder in a serious and sobering manner, replace them with those who can and will. Those people are out there. Doing nothing may, over time, bring a mass murderer to your shopping center, mall, church, movie theater, your child's school, etc. And you, your child or loved one might be present.

IT'S JOE BIDEN'S FAULT FOR THE NATION'S POLITICAL DIVISIVENESS: WHAT UTTER NONSENSE!

I am amazed at the number of social media posts that blame Joe Biden, and the Democrats in general, for the current divisiveness in America. According to right wing complainers, if only Biden and the Democrats would stop accusing folks of bigoted, racist, antisemitic statements that they make—some repeatedly--people would be unaware of differences and everyone would live in peace and harmony.

They evidently believe that the only time people are made aware of racial, ethnic, religious and other differences is when Democrats point them out the slurs.

The logical (if that's the right word here) extension of their railings against Biden and his supporters is that whatever vile, bigoted comments are uttered in public only matter when these speakers are called out for their despicable, anti-American utterances. This calling out and labeling, in turn, creates awareness of differences and allows feelings of supremacy on one hand, and inferiority on the other, to creep into the social conscience. This awareness, so these Biden critics say, is a direct result of the state of divisiveness, not the bigoted statements uttered in the first place.

In short, in their collective mind, everything would be kumbaya if only the Democrats would shut up. This position can be summed up in a single phrase: ignorance is bliss. This warped view turns logic and common sense on its ear.

I suppose these presumed intelligent, modern thinkers believe there is nothing wrong when a public official or public figure utters the most egregious comments against Blacks, Jews, Hispanics, Muslims, etc.; it's only when they're called to task that the problem of divisiveness rears its ugly head.

So, goes this nonsensical line, it's perfectly fine for Donald Trump to sing the praises of some "nice" neo-Nazis and white supremacists; it's fine when Kanye West rails against the Jews or when Trump invites West and another known antisemite for a bread-breaking social get-together. And it's perfectly fine for the right wing to cast out the LGBTQ community as societal outliers, just as it is reasonable and proper for them and their ilk to blame Antifa for the insurrection on January 6 at the nation's capital. (We know how far that last one went.)

But when these and other bigoted transgressions are called out by Biden and others, well, there you have the cause for all this division in America.

There aren't enough adjectives to properly describe the inanity and insanity of such a view.

Uttering a slur at a minority group member, or labeling an entire minority group with the most vicious condemnatory rants, is the personification of bigotry. Calling out bigotry is what decent, caring people do in their faithfulness to our democracy.

Those who hear those ugly words spoken should rise up in righteous indignation at this unconscionable treatment of fellow human beings.

We fought a Civil War and a world war over bigotry and hatred by self-proclaimed superior people against overpowered minorities.

Silence must never be the response to demonstrations of hatred. Recall the old adage: "The only thing necessary for the triumph of evil is for good men to do nothing."

It is the patriotic thing to call out bigotry regardless of form. There must never be a place for it in America. Bigotry is not what we're about. There must be harsh consequences for those who practice discrimination against, and intolerance of, others.

The preamble to our Constitution is clear: "We the People" includes all the citizens of the United States of America. The importance of this phrase shows that it wasn't just the framers of the Constitution or the legislators who were given powers to the government. Instead, the government gets all of its powers from the citizens of the United States of America. There is no qualifier in that quoted phrase. There is no limitation on its meaning.

When we pledge our allegiance to the flag of our country, we declare our universal acceptance of the principle "with liberty and justice for all." There is no qualifier either in the pledge.

Bigotry must never be met with silence. In recalling the great lyric of the past, "silence like a cancer grows." It is bigotry, hatred, prejudice, etc., that divides, not its calling out.

We must categorically reject any notion that Biden and the Democrats, by their calling out acts of bigotry, are responsible for the nation's divisions. Biden never did what Trump has been doing far too often over the past several years. It is Trump and his loyalists who, by their words, are fundamentally responsible for the divisions along racial, ethnic, religious and lifestyle lines, among others.

To eliminate as much as possible the heated rhetoric of hate, bigotry must be condemned in no uncertain terms. Those who divide must be called out as loudly and clearly as possible.

America is home to those who believe in the promise of a more perfect union; where we can live in peace in the land of the free and the home of the brave.

Prejudice, intolerance, discrimination, sexism--however bigotry may raise its ugly head--must never become acceptable here. People of goodwill must be vocal in assuring that this cancer on the public body is excised and relegated to the dustbin.

HOW DOES DONALD TRUMT REMAIN A POLITICAL FORCE DESPITE HIS BAD CONDUCT?

Since he burst onto the scene as a presidential candidate in 2015, Donald Trump has managed to criticize, condemn, belittle, etc., just about every community that makes up America, except white nationalists, evangelicals and those who otherwise believe he is their voice and speaks for them.

To his diehard loyalists, the MAGA people, he's uttered bigoted comments aimed at Muslims, Latin Americans, Asians, Jews, women, the LGBTQ communities---you name the group, he's demeaned it.

He's targeted former loyalists who withdrew their loyalty over his behavior; continues to belittle and criticize anyone who dares to question or challenge him; and doesn't seem to care what fires he ignites, so long as his base sticks with him.

And his base seems unmoved by his outrageous behavior as viewed through the eyes of the everyone else.

I can understand people who initially believed back in 2016 that this man who never previously held public or military office would bring his vast business knowledge and skills to the workings of government. But that has long ago been dispelled by the public record of his bogus business acumen.

I can understand people who believed they were ignored, talked down to, angered by a view that their hard-working efforts were unappreciated, and that too many were given free handouts over the years on the taxpayers' dime.

I understand the underlying notion—whether real or perceived--that government is the problem, in the words of Ronald Reagan. That government is too big, to heavy handed, taking too much of the rank-and-file workers' money and spending it on wasteful things. Whether or not there is merit to all of this, the fact is that, to many, perception is reality. I get that.

What I don't get are the folks who continue to give their undying support to Trump even after he's attacked in some manner or form just about every group that makes up the American tapestry.

Trump is facing most serious criminal investigations at both the state and federal levels for his conduct as a businessman, president and now former president. He's alienated many in his own party. His bigotry and bluster are there for all to see, yet his loyalists don't appear overly bothered by any of this; they just don't seem to care.

Republican elected officials seem of two points of view on Trump: either they fear his base and must remain silent, or they largely believe his words, while problematic or unfortunate, are not enough to toss down the gauntlet and declare that he doesn't represent the values of the Republican Party.

Whatever their reasons, they continue to give Trump a free hand even as he threatens to take the party down with him in 2024 if he's denied his party's nomination for president. The party leadership seems confident in the belief that Trump will self-destruct over the next several months. The risk to the party here should be a clear as a bell; Trump's supporters remain solid and, according to polls, won't be dissuaded even if he's indicted. Thus, the problem for the party's leaders is they don't seem to hear that bell ringing.

There is a third point that is too dangerous to deserve any credence—the possibility that they agree with his vile, spleen-venting ways; that they fully believe Trump is the victim, not the perpetrator. That it's the evil "them" that is the cause of all Trump's—and the right wing's—problems.

But what about his MAGA folks? Do they endorse Trump's bigoted statements? Do they share his views that provide cover for white supremacists and white nationalists? Do they agree with Kayne West's inane comments about Jews? Are they ok with Trump socializing with a known Holocaust denier?

If they don't support the bigoted comments, why don't they make that clear? Why don't they say they support Trump's policies, domestic and foreign, but not his language directed at women and minority groups?

Why stay silent if they don't have to? They can voice their support for all things Trump, but draw a line at overt bigotry.

The same can be said about the reaction of party leaders. Using such tepid words and "unfortunate," "in poor taste," etc., serves no useful purpose. There should be no shades of grey when it comes to bigoted conduct. In the absence of clear and vigorous condemnation, there is a vacuum which provides the source for aid and comfort for the bigot.

The sad, unalterable fact is that Trump himself could put an end to this by simply declaring in a clear and unmistakable manner that he opposes with all the vigor and strength he can muster any language or action that smacks of bigotry regardless of form. He could easily say he supports all Americans who favor inclusivity and unity, and that there is no room for division and hatred in America. He could conclude by saying he opposes any group that discriminates in any manner against other Americans. Sadly, we've yet to hear words like these uttered by him or his party loyalists.

Another sad fact is that if, say 50 years ago, anyone tried just a fraction of what Trump has gotten away with, that person wouldn't have made it to first base as a potential chief executive. We've certainly had our share of authoritarians and bigots, Sen. Joseph McCarthy and Gov. George Wallace come to mind. But McCarthy was ultimately discredited and shown the door, and Wallace actually saw the error of his ways and sought forgiveness after he was shot in an assassination attempt.

The fact is no one considers himself/herself to be a bigot. For them, it's really all about state's rights, fighting socialism on the left, paying less taxes, limited government, ending wasteful spending through useless programs, etc. They don't oppose minority groups per se; rather, they oppose the freebies, handouts and, in short, anything that smacks of favoritism directed toward these minority groups that they are paying for. Or so they say.

The simple fact is they can support all of those elements of Republican values; they can oppose those things they dislike; but draw a line in the sand when it comes to the kind of bigotry we've seen and heard over the past few years.

If, as they claim, they represent the "silent majority," then it's high time this "silent majority" spoke out in no uncertain terms that bigotry, prejudice, etc., have no place at the American table.

Let's hear them say it loud and clear. If they really mean it.

THE IMPORTANCE OF PETS IN OUR LIVES.

Each day I check my wife's and my Facebook page, we invariably find at least a couple of posts devoted to pets. The post might be about shirts worn by pet owners, or some comment about what a cat or dog did that was cute, funny or outlandish.

There are generally two types of pets: caged and roaming. Hamsters, gerbils, guinea pigs, mice, birds are caged; dogs and cats are the most prominent that roam through the house doing things dogs and cats do.

There have been books about how important pets are to our well-being, and it has been shown that you can judge the character of a person by how he/she treats an animal, particularly a dog or cat.

As a child, I didn't have any pets. They weren't allowed in the New York City brownstones and federal housing projects where I lived. It wasn't until I was on my own working as a news reporter in Fort Lauderdale that I had my first pet, a hamster.

After I married, settled down and had two children, it took my youngest daughter Amy to convince me to have a pet beyond the caged guinea pig, rabbit and mouse.

Amy worked as a vet tech and told us about a cat that needed a home. With some careful persistence on Amy's part, Rudy joined our family. Shortly thereafter, again with Amy's persistence, we took Jolly in as a rescue cat. Amy was also taking horse riding lessons from a woman who bred Shar-Peis. Mama shar-pei was about to deliver, and Amy was given the pick of the litter. I resisted, as I did rather timidly with the two cats, recalling my upbringing in New York where dogs growled and menaced the neighborhood, or so I believed. But Amy persisted again and I finally relented; Amy picked this adorable ball of dark fur that we named Pepper. The sale was sealed when I held this ball of fur and had this little tongue lick my face.

Rudy and Jolly were older male cats; very cuddly and affectionate. Pepper was born with conditions that are somewhat unique to the breed. The sad news for us was they don't live very long lives, usually about eight years or so.

Rudy and Jolly lived full lives, each passing at about 19. Pepper, thanks to the loving care and attention she received, survived to age 11.

After we lost our three pets, we vowed not to have anymore—until we visited our vet just a few days after we lost Pepper.

We saw two little balls of fur curled up together in the vet's front window. I asked my wife Harriet which one she wanted. She said we can't separate them, which I knew she would say. We took home a tan and black girl we named Sandy, and a dark, long-haired girl we named Mandy.

Our vet told us that there's a vast difference between boy and girl cats. We found that out rather quickly. Those of you familiar with this story know that girl cats are more particular and finicky than their male counterparts. If a female wants your attention, it's on her time, not yours.

So, we were back to two cats again. That was 11 years ago. They are still with us as independent as ever. They eat when they're hungry, even if they have to wake up Harriet to feed them. I get the job of moving them off my pillow when I want to lie down.

Two years ago, I wrote about how Moo and his sister, Floof, came into our lives and joined our family in November of 2020, when they were barely two months old. We never had kittens at such a young age, and we enjoyed how the two of them played together, scampering through the house, jumping from chair to table to counter (driving our two older cats to distraction), curious about their surroundings, getting into everything, and generally doing all things little kittens do.

We were now a family of four felines, three girls and one boy.

Shortly after we brought them home, we took them to our vet for examination and kitty shots. And then we received devastating news that Moo tested positive for feline leukemia. Prognosis is 3-5 years.

We vowed that we would give Moo the best life we could, making sure he got the best medical care available.

A few weeks later, Moo had an attack. He was gasping for air and threw up. But it passed that day, he resumed kitten antics, and we thought nothing further about it. However, the next day, he had another attack, only this time he ejected mucous. We immediately made an appointment with our vet and took Moo in for examination, including an x-ray.

When we saw the x-ray, we were shocked. A huge baseball-size lymphoma had formed in Moo's chest cavity and was pressing on his esophagus; he was at risk for suffocation.

The doctor said surgery was out; he wouldn't survive that. Chemo and steroids wouldn't reduce the size of the tumor. The vet didn't have to tell us about options; we could see in her eyes what had to be done.

Harriet and I were devastated. A few hours ago, Moo was an active little kitten. Now, we had but a few precious moments to say goodbye.

Moo had given us so much joy and laughter. He was the ringleader of our four felines. He made our two senior cats stare in wonder as he frolicked through our home; and his frequent tussles with his sister delighted us, giving one another a lifetime playmate. Or so we thought.

Through our sobs and tears, Harriet held Moo in her arms, and I petted him as the vet injected him. Moo let out a yelp and then fell still. After a second injection, which Moo didn't feel, she checked his breathing and said he was gone.

As we have done for our previous three pets that we lost, we had him cremated, ordered a stone and buried him next to them. Moo's stone carries this message that is all so true: "pawprints on our hearts."

Losing Moo was different. While Pepper, Rudy and Jolly lived full lives, Moo was with us only 2 ½ months. Our first three pets were ill and at the end of their lives; we had time to say our goodbyes. Moo was active and full of life even on his last day, when we were faced with the grim reality that his genetic line deprived our little one of his life. We now know all too well the pain of losing such a small, loving pet at such a young age.

But as pets do, Moo taught us something about ourselves. In fact, each of our pets taught us this great lesson. They are God's little creatures who give us unrequited love in return for what is hoped will be loving and caring owners. Studies have shown that pet ownership is good for one's mental and emotional health. They help reduce stress and keep you engaged. They are wonderful companions.

We know Moo never had chance; that x-ray told us his life was over. But it doesn't lessen the pain of losing a pet we loved, especially one so young and full of life.

As for Floof, since our older cats live in their own orbit, Moo's sister gets plenty of love and attention whenever she allows us to give it. She is the most curious cat I've ever seen, and isn't afraid when someone knocks on our door or comes in to visit us. Mandy and Sandy scamper off and hide under the bed in our bedroom.

Yes, it hurts to lose a pet, and since they don't live as long as we do, losing a pet is part of life. But while they're with us, they teach us about love and devotion, and how fragile life is. There really is no greater lesson.

PERFECTING THE PLAN.

The Florida Republican Party well knows that the goal of any political party is power, for with power comes control.

Since the 1990s, the state Republican Party has been making steady inroads toward the ultimate prize: absolute power.

Since the beginning of this century, no Democrat has occupied the governor's chair. The governor, however, has had to contend with Democrats in the cabinet and until a few years ago, with a Democrat in the U.S. Senate.

No more.

The Florida Legislature was split, with Republicans in control, but without the ability to neuter the Democrats as a political force.

No more.

Beginning in January, the governor and entire state cabinet will be in Republican hands. The state house of representatives will be split 85-35 in favor of the Republicans. The state senate will be split 28-12 in favor of the Republicans. With this supermajority in excess of the 2/3 vote standard, the Republican Party will be able to pass virtually anything without the Democrats' ability to block it. They will have the power to override any gubernatorial veto (not that this will be a barrier for a Republican governor) and change the rules of the house and senate as they see fit.

All the Democrats will have is their voice; they will have no power. They will get only what the Republicans decide to give them.

You can bet the mortgage that, with control of two-thirds of the three branches of government, Republicans will set their sights on the entirety of the state judiciary.

The governor will work diligently to fill the several judicial nominating commissions with like-minded people who, in turn, will choose like-minded lawyers to fill county, circuit, and appellate courts.

As these judicial positions are filled, the Republican Party will take aim at opposition voices. Already Florida officials are seeking new tools to silence dissent and prevent demonstrations at the State Capitol. These tools are in the form of what they euphemistically call <u>freedom of speech rules proposed</u> by the state Department of Management Services, the agency that serves as the state's property manager.

DMS wants to empower law enforcement to remove individuals they think may prove disruptive from traditional public forum arenas — such as the fourth floor rotunda separating the Florida House and Senate chambers, and the Capitol Courtyard.

This proposal says that, "Because the Capitol Complex is often a destination for children learning about their State government," individuals can be removed from the premises and charged with trespassing when law enforcement believes:

- Displays and sounds are gratuitous and indecent,
- Material arouses prurient interests,
- They likely will create disturbances or unusual noise,
- Their behavior will create a hazard or disruption to performance of official duties.

Think of the amount of power this vests in law enforcement. There are no clear standards involved here, just someone's judgment.

Republicans know that to assure complete control by the exercise of complete power, dissent must be quelled—and this is just the beginning.

If the judiciary concludes that these restrictions on free speech are valid—which is one salient purpose of having a like-minded judiciary—what is to prevent the Republicans from imposing these restrictions on other places where people congregate?

The legal principle involved here is called the public forum doctrine. This doctrine is an analytical method used by the courts in First Amendment cases to determine the constitutionality of speech restrictions imposed on government property. Courts employ this doctrine to decide whether groups should have access to engage in expressive activities on such property.

Florida's state capital is considered a limited public forum where people gather for a presumed limited purpose—in this instance, government participation in some way or form. This limited public forum is in contrast to a public street or roadway where people gather in general.

However, what is to prevent future courts from expanding this limited public forum to places more generally used by the public, under a claim that the protests somehow fit within the four categories noted above, or others enacted along these same lines?

Restricting places where people can protest is one aspect of quelling dissent.

Another is instilling fear of speaking out by punishing dissenters by means other than trespassing; that is, more severe punishment. Assigning the legitimacy of protest to the eye and ear of the beholder is a slippery slope. What's one person's peaceful protest is another's perceived violent protest. And a like-minded judge may be unsympathetic to the protesters' First Amendment rights.

Going forward, Florida will serve as a model for the other state Republican parties, and the party's national officeholders as well.

With the sea of red that has washed over the state, others will look to Florida to see how Republicans can replicate their takeover elsewhere.

The Republicans had a great chance from 2017-2019 when they controlled the executive and legislative branches of the federal government. However, they didn't have a chief executive schooled in navigating the intricacies of government.

With a more palatable Republican in the White House, and both houses of Congress in Republican hands, the party's ability to put more judges on the federal bench and adopt favored policies that will withstand judicial review will be greater than it was not too long ago. The party leadership made notes, and now they want to complete the task according to their takeover plan. Next time, they say, they'll get it right. Perhaps far right.

And history will once again repeat itself.

INTERMINORITY DISCRIMINATION PLAYS INTO A "DIVIDE AND CONQUER" MENTALITY.

The recent attacks on Jews by rapper Kanye West (Ye) and comic David Chappelle raise an issue that should alarm all American minorities because it plays into the hands of a "divide and conquer" mentality.

What is so shocking is that the antisemitic attacks come from two African-Americans who would go ballistic if the shoe were on the other foot. If either of these men, or African American citizens as a whole, were the subject of racial slurs, their reactions would be predictable and well justified. But their fail or refuse to see a double standard when they attack another minority group. In short, it's ok to point the finger; it's outrageous when the finger is pointed at them.

Just today, Ye commented that the reason he hasn't enjoyed support from other entertainers for his bigoted remarks is because they're "controlled." With each passing comment, Ye demonstrates he has serious mental health issues. Yet, because of fame and notoriety, he enjoys mass media coverage for every outlandish, outrageous comment he makes. This recalls that line from the song "If I Were a Rich Man" from "Fiddler on the Roof"--"When you're rich, they think you really know." (The irony of the relevance here of this lyric from a play about a Jewish family facing discrimination and living in troubled times is not lost on me.)

The fact is just because someone is wealthy doesn't make him/her a genius, or even reasonably smart. A stupid man who inherits millions is still a stupid man. Wealth confers no intelligence. While there is something to be said about the relationship between intelligence and gaining wealth, intelligence is more than business or financial knowledge, or perhaps being smart enough to be managed by intelligent marketers and promoters; intelligence also considers one's ability to engage in critical thinking, use logic and analytical reasoning, etc., from a background of history, English, science, math, etc.

Ye's ability to become a wealthy man takes some smarts; his bigoted statements, however, reveal much about his overall intelligence and level of knowledge. The same can be said of others who are perhaps smart enough to make lots of money, but stupid enough to make outlandish statements based on opinion devoid of fact.

To be sure, interminority discrimination is nothing new. A recent discussion on this subject shows there has long been competition and racial prejudice between African Americans and Latino Americans. There have also been inter-racial tensions between African Americans and Asian Americans.

Changing demographics is one major cause. It's important to understand these tensions because they must be overcome, as circumstances over the past few years amply demonstrate.

"Tensions Between African Americans and Latino Americans.

With the growth of the Latino American in the United States, there are areas of competition for housing, jobs and other resources with African Americans. Tensions in communities have also been reflected in racial tensions between these ethnic groups in prisons. In several significant riots in California prisons, for instance, Latino and black inmates targeted each other over racial issues. There have been reports of racially motivated attacks by gangs against

African Americans who have moved into neighborhoods occupied mostly by Hispanic Americans, and vice versa.

Tensions Between African-Americans and Jewish Americans

African Americans and Jewish Americans have interacted throughout much of the history of the United States. This relationship has included widely publicized cooperation and conflict, and—since the 1970s—has been an area of significant academic research. Cooperation during the Civil Rights Movement was strategic and significant, culminating in the Civil Rights Act of 1964.

The relationship has also featured conflict and controversy related to such topics as the Black Power movement, Zionism, affirmative action, and the antisemitic canard (rumor or unfounded charge) concerning the alleged role of American and Caribbean-based Jews in the Atlantic slave trade.

Tensions between African Americans and Asian Americans

Despite African Americans and Asian Americans each having suffered from racial prejudice in the United States, some of their people have uneasy relations with the other ethnic group. Because of the centuries of abuses from historic slavery and its aftermath, discussions of racial tension in the United States have often focused on black-white relations. This has failed to include the perspective of Asian Americans in the racial discourse.

Some Asian Americans feel stuck in limbo, as they have had differences and suffered discrimination from each of these other ethnic groups. At the same time, Asian Americans have been extolled as the "model minority", because of their record of achievement and statistically high reported educational scores and incomes. But not all are equally successful. While these two groups have both faced historical and current racial discrimination from whites, the forms of discrimination have taken diverse forms. In addition, these two groups (which encompass numerous ancestral backgrounds) have also competed for jobs, education and resources over the decades, and have displayed tensions toward each other."

This brief narrative gives some basic understanding of these tensions, and it is well known that the first step toward solving a problem is to admit there is one, and then finding ways to eliminate it to the best of one's abilities.

If a group fears that it's rapidly becoming less and less of a majority, how could it go about preventing this from ever happening? The answer should be self-evident: by the old saw of "divide and conquer." If minority groups wage battles among themselves, this allows the single diminishing majority group to seize and maintain the upper hand.

At a time when white nationalist and white supremacy organizations get so much media play, it seems prudent for minority groups—particularly those under attack by these organizations, and other individuals and groups as well—to explore areas of common interests and agree to speak as one should any one of them be attacked In other words, an attack on one is an attack on all; sort of a NATO pact among America's minority citizens. Recall the Bible says "where there is unity there is strength."

The goal should be a realization that, although there are group differences (race, culture, ethnicity, etc.) we are now all Americans under one Constitution, one flag and one overriding commitment to a form of government hatched by immigrants fleeing persecution almost 250 years ago. Whatever the friction might be is outweighed by the ties that bind.

This can be accomplished. It takes courage and commitment.

A DIALOGUE ON THE FIRST AMENDMENT'S FREEDOM OF SPEECH, RIGHT TO ASSEMBLE AND PETITION FOR REDRESS FROM GRIEVANCES.

(In an earlier post, I commented on Florida officials "seeking new tools to silence dissent and prevent demonstrations at the State Capitol. These tools are in the form of what they euphemistically call freedom of speech rules proposed by the state Department of Management Services, the agency that serves as the state's property manager.

DMS wants to empower law enforcement to remove individuals they think may prove disruptive from traditional public forum arenas — such as the fourth floor rotunda separating the Florida House and Senate chambers, and the Capitol Courtyard.

This proposal says that, "Because the Capitol Complex is often a destination for children learning about their State government," individuals can be removed from the premises and charged with trespassing when law enforcement believes:

- Displays and sounds are gratuitous and indecent,
- Material arouses prurient interests,
- They likely will create disturbances or unusual noise,
- Their behavior will create a hazard or disruption to performance of official duties.

Think of the amount of power this vests in law enforcement. There are no standards involved here, just someone's judgment.

Republicans know that to assure complete control by the exercise of complete power, dissent must be quelled—and this is just the beginning.

If the judiciary concludes that these restrictions on free speech are valid—which is one salient purpose of having a like-minded judiciary—what is to prevent the Republicans from imposing these restrictions on other places where people congregate?

The legal principle involved here is called the public forum doctrine. This doctrine is an analytical method used by the courts in First Amendment cases to determine the constitutionality of speech restrictions imposed on government property. Courts employ this doctrine to decide whether groups should have access to engage in expressive activities on such property.

Florida's state capital is considered a limited public forum where people gather for a presumed limited purpose—in this instance, government participation in some way or form. This limited public forum is in contrast to a public street or roadway where people gather in general.

However, what is to prevent future courts from expanding this limited public forum to places more generally used by the public, under a claim that the protests somehow fit within the four categories noted above, or others enacted along these same lines?

Restricting places where people can protest is one aspect of quelling dissent.

Another is instilling fear of speaking out by punishing dissenters by means other than trespassing; that is, more severe punishment.

Assigning the legitimacy of protest to the eye and ear of the beholder is a slippery slope. What's one person's peaceful protest is another's perceived violent protest.

And a like-minded judge may be unsympathetic to the protesters' First Amendment rights."

A noted Tallahassee-based reporter and columnist took issue with my comments regarding efforts by Florida Gov. Ron DeSantis to deal with demonstrations at the state Capitol. Because of the importance of this First Amendment issue, I am setting out his comments and my responses.)

"I don't see a problem here. You know, it really is possible to express views civilly and politely. There's no constitutional guarantee that we can scream in people's faces. If 100 nude people wanted to demonstrate in the Capitol's 4th floor rotunda, would the state be obligated to allow it? If some white supremacists wanted to shout the N-word and chant antisemitic slogans, would legislators have to let them disrupt meetings? I understand friendly persuasion doesn't work, but that doesn't give us the right to use force."

I've litigated many First Amendment cases, and if the issues were as you describe, I would fully agree with you, but in free speech cases, it's not the black-and-white that is of concern; it's the many shades of grey. Legislative acts, including rules, must be such as to clearly inform of the conduct both permitted and prohibited.

With regard to the points noted by DMS, there is entirely too many holes that must be filled; too much discretion in decision-making. For example, what is a matter that is both gratuitous and indecent? When does a gathering reach the level of the likelihood of creating a "disturbance or unusual noise?" And what exactly is an "unusual noise?" Does someone bumping into the arm of another constitute a disturbance? To some folks, it could. If someone slips and falls, is that an unusual noise? And does this constitute a likelihood of creating a disturbance? To someone not used to such things, it could. A disturbance or unusual noise left to the eye and ear of the beholder's personal judgment creates serious free speech issues stemming from the very real risk of selective enforcement.

Finally, what criteria will be used in determining when a peaceful protest "create(s) a hazard or disruption to performance of official duties?" Again, too much is left to the individual and creates impermissible selective performance issues.

Such rules are designed to do one thing: create fear in those who want to engage in constitutionally protected speech in the most significant location where government policies are formulated. If the intent was to truly address when a peaceful protest crosses the line, there are far better--and perfectly constitutional--ways to accomplish this rather than these open-ended phrases that vest the decision solely in the discretion of law enforcement.

(Another commentator asked what suggestion he has for dealing with this. This is his response.)

"I'd suggest everyone remain civil. If your side loses, you lose. Go win some elections. Get a governor and legislators who'll operate the way you like. Nothing -- nothing -- justifies

deliberately offensive conduct or any threat of violence. The civil rights marchers in Birmingham 1963 are remembered with respect and accomplished their goal; the Oath Keepers who invaded the U.S. Capitol last year are not respected and did not accomplish what they wanted. There's a reason for that."

Unfortunately, civility as you might contemplate might not match civility as interpreted by others. Peaceful protest is a form of civil disobedience, but once again, there are those pesky shades of grey that lead to court decisions. There is plenty of caselaw out there that discusses the parameters of civil or peaceful protests, civil disobedience, and when these actions cross over the line. I suggest that the drafters of this rule, and any legislation that follows, check with constitutional First Amendment law experts.

That's the same amendment that, in addition to free speech and assembly, allows for petitioning for redress of government. And where better to accomplish all three than at the location where laws are made. We are talking about core political speech, the highest form of protected speech. This is why rules implicating these rights must be written in the most precise manner possible. The purpose of this precision in draftsmanship is to avoid any shade of grey.

"Individual events will have shades of grey but I don't see any difficulty when speech becomes conduct. Standing on the sidewalk with a sign saying "Stop the Steal" is protected speech, charging into the Capitol and screaming "Hang

Mike Pence" is not. If the protestors against the "Don't Say Gay" law assemble in the courtyard with signs and speeches, fine, and if they enter the House chamber and calmly watch the debate, that's their right. If they become disruptive, the Capitol cops have a duty to remove them."

I have no problem with any of your examples. But if they enter the Capitol, chances are those in charge aren't going to give protestors a round of applause for exercising their constitutional rights. More likely they will be looking for that first statement or action they can fit under one or more of those broad descriptions and start moving them out, with violence if law enforcement deems necessary. The free speech/assembly/petition process must be considered in light of current dynamics.

There is a real and serious tension between those who will do whatever they can to restrict these rights, while others will do whatever they can to exercise them. Democracy is loud, often boisterous and on occasion ugly. But it's the best government we have.

IT'S ALL COMING OUT IN THE WASH.

Let's see now.

The House January 6 investigating committee goes out of business the end of this month. However, it will issue its final report and release all testimony and evidence before then.

The report will be written mostly by the four committee members who are real lawyers, not the outrageous kind who represented Donald Trump—and still do. (Several of those lawyers should be very concerned about their own conduct, both from a criminal law standpoint and their standings in their respective regulatory bar associations.

Predictably, the report will be greeted by Trump and his acolytes as a partisan hatchet job, ignoring the fact that Kevin McCarthy barred Republicans from serving on the committee but despite that, two of the nine committee members are Republicans. Although Reps. Kinzinger and Cheney are leaving Congress, they view Trump as anything but a traditional Goldwater-Reagan Republican. In fact, they view him much like many Republicans do now--as a clear and present threat to our democracy. And no doubt more Republicans will join Democrats who knew this from the get-go.

The Trump diehards will also ignore the fact that a wealth of testimony and evidence comes from Republicans, including those who worked for Trump in the White House.

But ignorance of Trump's peccadillos is one of his loyalists' strong points.

(Trump's House Republican supporters vow to investigate this committee. That should be a real donnybrook, as Democrats will undoubtedly have in their report those transgressions by some of the House Republicans. Dueling investigations recall one important message: be careful what you wish for.)

Those portions of the report that implicate criminal conduct—and there is plenty of that—will be forwarded to the Department of Justice, which is already conducting its own investigation into Trump's transgressions under the auspices of a special counsel.

Then there's that trial in New York against the Trump organization; and after a years' long losing fight, a House committee is finally examining Trump's tax returns over the past six years covering that period immediately before and during his term in office.

And a federal appeals court made up of three Republican judges, two appointed by Trump, rejected the appointment of a special master sought by him and ordered by a Trump-appointed trial judge in connection with his illegal removal of government records from the White House to Mar-a-Lago. This means the investigation into Trump's action will be undertaken in toto by the FBI and Department of Justice.

Then there are those ongoing and nearly completed investigations in Georgia and New York.

Did I miss any?

There don't appear to be additional rabbits Trump can pull out of the hat to delay the inevitability of accountability. This doesn't mean his lawyers, at least the ones who are left, won't try some maneuver. If they're efforts are like the papers his lawyers filed contesting the election and beyond, any last-ditch efforts will likewise be laughed out of court.

Meanwhile, Trump continues to press on with his candidacy for 2024. To make sure the coast is clear for him, he has, as is typical for him, attached silly, juvenile labels to his prospective opponents like Florida Gov. Ron DeSantis, who's at least savvy enough not to similarly respond. Trump's done this labelling to just about every Republican who at one time or another supported him, like Mitch McConnell, Ted Cruz, Lindsey Graham, the list goes on and on. Some have even gone back to supporting him, even though Trump has no ability to impact their re-election bids in the near future.

Trump has also ingratiated himself with his base by entertaining Kanye West (Ye) and his avowed antisemitism; and Nicholas Fuentes, a 24-year-old white supremacist, antisemite and Holocaust denier. Such wonderful, caring people to pal around with. Of course, Trump says he doesn't know Fuentes, but Ye does. Imagine that; Ye knows something Trump doesn't. But Trump does know Ye and his bigotry. Ye is reported to have asked Trump to be his running mate in 2024; what chutzpah!

That's a lot of serious stuff on Trump's plate. Lots of information about which we know only in bits and pieces, or based on speculation, or what we witnessed during the televised committee hearings this past summer, will be set out in full without Republican loyalists' efforts to befuddle, confuse or gaslight.

If Trump thought 2022 was a tough year, wait until he gets a load of 2023.

(This is a column I wrote for the Tallahassee Democrat a couple of years ago that is relevant today.)

AMERICA ALREADY HAS SOCIALIST PROGRAMS—YOU PROBABLY BENEFIT FROM THEM.

Conservatives label any progressive legislation offered by the Democrats as "socialism." Stripped of the emotive gloss, here is the reality they avoid, either through indifference or ignorance.

First, the United States — like every other country with an advanced economy, such as the United Kingdom, Germany, France and Japan — is already a partly socialist country, with a mixed economy and many government programs that deal with the public good.

Social Security is a "socialist" program: It's a government-run pension system that cuts out private money managers. Medicare — a single-payer, government-run health insurance program for those over 65 – is, also.

"Medicare For All" would simply extend this to the rest of the population.

Second, the minimum wage, maximum hour and child labor laws that go back more than a century are likewise "socialist" programs, in that the government intervenes in the capitalist market to require employers to meet minimum standards that might not be met in a pure, unregulated "free" market.

Agricultural and energy subsidies are likewise socialist programs. There are others as well.

The real debate isn't between capitalism and socialism, but about the appropriate balance between the two. Conservatives want to reduce Social Security and Medicare benefits and lessen the numbers who qualify, while progressives want to increase and expand these programs. Many progressives want to move towards a Medicare system covering all Americans, not just those over 65, while centrist Democrats want to protect the Affordable Care Act, which is a hybrid between private insurance and government insurance and regulation; conservatives want to go back to the all-private system that pre-dated the ACA.

The bottom line here is that government already supports higher education (that's socialism) but progressives want to make a public college education free or debt-free. Conservatives support government subsidies for agriculture and the oil energy (that's socialism) while many progressives believe this is "reverse welfare" for the rich and want to reduce them.

THE FREE STATE OF FLORIDA.

I can see this joint statement from Gov. Ron DeSantis and his legislative loyalists in the not-too-distant future:

"Florida is the freest state in America.

In the recent past, we've given all Floridians the freedom of a 15-week abortion ban; freedom of what can't be taught to our children about sexuality and racial history; freedom from expansive college courses of study; and freedom from those pesky congressional minority-access districts. We will continue to dedicate ourselves to freeing Floridians from anything that causes uncomfortable feelings, sadness or discomfort.

Yet, there are those ungrateful, noisy people who don't appreciate your freedoms we've provided. They want to protest all the good things we've done for you, and want to prevent the good, decent Floridians like you from telling us what a great job we're doing, and how happy you are to live in such a free and glorious state.

So. we've taken some minor steps to assure your easy access to the Capitol. We will not allow your voices of gratitude to be silenced or shouted down. We don't want---and we know you don't want—to hear a lot of angry people telling you and us that we're wrong. You know that we know what's best for you. We know the last thing you want is to doubt your great wisdom in knowing the great job we're doing for you.

If a protestor gets too loud or rambunctious, as determined by our law enforcement officers, they will be taken from the Capitol and charged with trespassing on government property.

If these disrespectful protestors can't stand idly by and let the good and decent citizens offer their praise to your elected leaders and allow us to pass laws that further demonstrate our commitment to your freedom, we will take further action to assure that your will is met.

Our loyal and dedicated citizens deserve easy and unrestricted access to the Capitol, whether by walking or driving. To assure that there is no shouting or other actions as determined by law enforcement that affects free public access to show appreciation for our great leadership in providing you with such freedom, we will establish a one-mile zone around the Capitol in which these rabble-rousers will be barred from engaging in such disloyal and disrespectful conduct. This will ensure that no citizen and voter has to tolerate such bad behavior from these complainers and naysayers.

This is what true freedom is all about in the Free State of Florida."

Printed in the United States
by Baker & Taylor Publisher Services